CRAFTING TRADITIONS

CRAFTING TRADITIONS

The Architecture of Mark Lemmon

RICHARD R. BRETTELL & WILLIS CECIL WINTERS

New photography by Carolyn Brown

MEADOWS MUSEUM
FINE ART

SMU PRESS
2005

This publication and the exhibition that it accompanies were made possible by the Meadows Foundation of Texas and Dr. and Mrs. Mark Lemmon.

The authors would like to thank the following individuals and institutions for their assistance in the preparation of this volume: Rachel Roberts, Archives Director, Dallas Historical Society; Diane Gallagher, University Archivist, Boston University; Joan Gosnell, University Archivist, Southern Methodist University, Dallas; Rev. Gary Denning, First Baptist Church of Pittsburgh; Becky Riley, First Presbyterian Church, Wichita Falls; Warren Griffin, First United Church of San Angelo; Jessamine Younger, Archivist, Highland Park United Methodist Church, Dallas; and Keitha Lowrance, Dallas.

Published by:
Meadows Museum
Southern Methodist University
5900 Bishop Boulevard
Dallas, TX 75275-0357

Southern Methodist University Press
P.O. Box 750415
Dallas, TX 75275-0415

Coordinating Editor: Courtney E. Kennedy
Design by: Tom Dawson, Dallas
Printed and bound by: CS Graphics, Inc., Singapore

LIBRARY OF CONGRESS CATALOGING-IN-PUBLICATION DATA

Crafting traditions : the architecture of Mark Lemmon / edited by Richard R. Brettell ; with essays by Richard R. Brettell, Willis Winters.
    p. cm.
    Includes bibliographical references and index.
    ISBN 0-87074-495-X
    1. Lemmon, Mark, 1889-1975–Criticism and interpretation. 2. Lemmon, Mark, 1889-1975–Catalogs. 3. Historicism in architecture–Texas–Dallas. 4. Architecture–Texas–Dallas–20th century. I. Brettell, Richard R. II. Winters, Willis.

NA737.L44C73 2005
726'.092–dc22
                                          2004064988

Frontispiece: *Stairwell in Perkins Chapel*, Southern Methodist University, Dallas, 1947–1951.

CONTENTS

Edmund P. Pillsbury

MARK LEMMON (1889–1975) was the most important historicist architect of twentieth-century Dallas. Although others built Georgian, Tudor, Spanish Colonial, and Louis XVI houses in the city, Lemmon was unique in bringing a deep knowledge of European architectural history to all aspects of the city's heritage. When he arrived in Dallas from World War I in 1919, the city had a decidedly provincial, heavily beaux arts character—massive columns, swags, moldings, and podiums adorned the best houses, churches, and public buildings. When he retired from practice in the 1960s, he had designed churches, public and private schools, university buildings, municipal buildings, and private houses of a refinement and intelligence completely new to the city.

This volume accompanies the first of a series of exhibitions at the Meadows Museum devoted to twentieth-century architecture in Dallas/Fort Worth and the larger region. With a handsome lead gift from the architect's son and daughter-in-law, Dr. and Mrs. Mark Lemmon, the series proposes to investigate the major architects and design issues from Dallas's most important century. Future exhibitions, likewise accompanied by monographic publications, will be devoted to the careers of O'Neil Ford in North Texas, Howard Meyer, and George Dahl. The Lemmon undertaking focuses on two major themes: the architecture of public education, in particular the extensive work done by Mark Lemmon and his firm for the Dallas Independent School District and the Port

Fig. 1
Portrait of Mark Lemmon, c. 1950.

Arthur School District between 1926 and 1962; and "historicism," or the kind of modern architecture that takes architectural history as its source material and that roots modern buildings in the civic traditions of European urban architecture from Greco-Roman times through the eighteenth century.

Dr. Richard R. Brettell, Adjunct Senior Curator of the Meadows Museum and Margaret McDermott Professor of Aesthetic Studies at the University of Texas, Dallas, deserves credit for introducing the concept of a Lemmon exhibition and publication as the first in a series devoted to the practice of architecture in Dallas in the early- and mid-twentieth century. A prolific architectural historian and critic, Professor Brettell has contributed a valuable essay defining the context for the appreciation of the historicist architecture of Mark Lemmon. His words perfectly complement the critical biography compiled by the architect and noted historian Willis Cecil Winters, AIA, whose text chronicles the life and career of Mark Lemmon in a lucid and evocative fashion and places our knowledge of the architect and his extensive body of work on a factual basis in print for the first time. The beautiful new photography of Lemmon's finest surviving projects was commissioned from Carolyn Brown, one of the country's leading architectural photographers, while the supervision of the design and printing of this volume, published in conjunction with SMU Press, was entrusted to Tom Dawson, one of the foremost members of the design profession worldwide.

AN INTRODUCTION TO MARK LEMMON
An Historicist Architect in the Modernist Century

Richard R. Brettell

When Mark Lemmon graduated from architecture school in 1916, modern architecture had already been born. With its American center firmly planted in Chicago, modernism in architecture had produced major masterpieces of commercial, residential, and institutional architecture—most of which had no specific prototypes in the history of European architecture. No "historical" buildings allowed a viewer to explain Louis Sullivan's Auditorium Building, Frank Lloyd Wright's Unity Temple, or the same architect's Robie House. These buildings boldly asserted a new architectural future based on new technology, rethought ideas of living, progressive values, and future-driven thinking. This brand of American modernism was combined in the 1920s, the first decade of Lemmon's practice in Dallas, with a European-led architectural practice that came to be called the "International Style," which decried any form of historicism. "Modern Architecture," for its greatest practitioners in America and Europe, was not driven by local or national traditions, which had been rendered obsolete by the railroad, the telegraph, the motorcar, and other high-speed linkages that seemed radically to shrink the world.

These new modes of architectural expression were immediately embraced by architectural theorists, critics, and historians, and by the 1930s, particularly with the publications and exhibitions of the new Architecture and Design Department of the Museum of Modern Art, modernism *was* architecture. If the World's Fairs of 1893 in Chicago and 1900 in Paris were vast exercises in architectural historicism—with miles of columns, swags, and pilasters—those of 1933 in Chicago and 1939 in New York were almost completely ahistorical, or "modern." And, when the Museum of Modern Art opened its new building in 1939, it had no historical ornament that could be associated with any of the traditional museum buildings, palaces, or temples of

Plate 1
Detail of light and trim on
Alex W. Spence Junior High School,
Dallas, 1938–1940.

the past. Indeed, MOMA, as we call it today, looked more like a department store of the future than anyone's idea of a museum in 1939.

However, when we actually look at American cities in historical photographs from the first half of the twentieth century, it is perfectly obvious that modernism in architecture was employed in a distinct minority of buildings. Modern buildings even in New York and Chicago, far from dominating the visual environment, actually blended into American urban historicist zones. Together with Gothic, Romanesque, Palladian, Queen Anne, Georgian, Tudor, Louis XV, or Regency, Modern buildings had their own distinctive style. Flat roofs, honest expression of materials, liberal amounts of glass, opening of corners, flowing spaces, and absence of ornament—all these and other qualities of form came to be associated with Modern buildings. The men and women who built them were future-oriented and progressive, while their friends and colleagues who built variously historicist buildings valued tradition, history, and knowledge.

This was certainly true of Mark Lemmon's Dallas. Although a native Texan, Lemmon had "gone east" to attend architecture school in Boston, Massachusetts, which, unlike Chicago, was part of an intensely traditional metropolitan area still dominated by European historicist architecture. Even the new urbanism of the Back Bay and the wonderful parks along the Fenways designed by Frederick Law Olmsted were rooted in the past—either in Georgian London for the Back Bay or the informal pastoral landscapes of eighteenth-century English designer Capability Brown for Olmsted's Fenways. The Boston area viewed itself as a bastion of European

civilization in a New America, not as a place on the frontier, as did brash young Chicago. And the greatest architect of nineteenth-century Boston, Henry Hobson Richardson, had graduated from the Ecole des Beaux Arts in Paris and was one of the most sophisticated historicist architects in our nation's history. Thus, for Lemmon as a student in the Boston area before the arrival of the modernists in the late 1930s, architecture itself was rooted in a deep knowledge of the human architectural past, even as it was taught at the Massachusetts Institute of Technology, founded in Boston in 1865.

In Lemmon's first year at MIT, the university made a decision to move from its nineteenth-century buildings in old Boston to ample newly acquired property across the Charles River in Cambridge. After considering Désiré Despradelle, a French-born member of the MIT architecture faculty (and Lemmon's teacher), and Cass Gilbert, who had worked to design the campus of the University of Minnesota and was to design the first master plan for the University of Texas, the university selected a French-trained, Boston-based architect, William Welles Bosworth, to design the campus. Bosworth created the grandest and most architecturally consistent campus then in existence, planning a single huge building with two Pantheonic domes and wings of dressed limestone in Versailles-like proportion given form by beautifully detailed sequences of Ionic columns and pilasters (figure 2). The planning, building, and moving of the campus were the major events of Lemmon's years at MIT, and the entire university moved to Cambridge just after his graduation in 1916. This lengthy process also gave the Texan both a real understanding of vast building

Fig. 2
*First building of new campus,
Massachusetts Institute of Technology,*
Boston, 1916, William Welles
Bosworth, New York.

projects for educational institutions and a familiarity with Boston-based educational theory, both of which were to serve him well in Texas.

Lemmon took the train back to Dallas in 1919. He arrived in a city that seemed on the verge of another boom. Downtown Dallas had a series of new buildings, constructed in the years he had been in Boston and Europe. Perhaps the best-known today is the Adolphus Hotel (figure 3), completed in 1913 and designed by the St. Louis firm of Barnett, Haynes, & Barnett to bring a new level of opulence to Texas. Although the building is often described as Second Empire and related to the Plaza Hotel in New York, it is actually rooted in the Italianate

Baroque architecture of seventeenth-century Flanders and Holland—a decidedly northern take on Italy. And, in this case, it is clear that, for the Dallas public, these historicist subtleties meant little. Indeed, the building promoted a sense of substantial culture and luxury without being encumbered by the particular cultural meanings of its historical allusions. And, if we consider this building in the context of the other classical monuments built for religion (the Gaston Avenue Baptist Church of 1904, figure 4, or the Third Temple Emanu-el of 1917, figure 5), public life, or residence (the Thorpe House, Lakeside Drive, 1915, figure 6), we are confronted by a provincial American city that looked to St. Louis, New York, London, and Rome for its architectural allusions. The modernism of Chicago was very little in evidence in the Dallas to which Mark Lemmon returned in 1919.

If Europe—particularly London, Paris, and Rome—was already paramount as the cultural and historical prototype for the cultivated American city

Fig. 3
Adolphus Hotel, Dallas, 1913, Barnett, Haynes, & Barnett, St. Louis.

Fig. 4
Gaston Avenue Baptist Church, Dallas, 1904, C.W. Bulger and Son.

in 1916, this inevitable Eurocentrism became even more pronounced after World War I. No matter how traumatic the war was for Americans—its trenches, nauseous gases, camouflaged military encampments, aerial bombardments, and the like—it was also the first time that many lower and middle-class American men were able actually to visit Europe, to experience one or two of its historical cities, to move through landscapes inhabited for millennia, to confront directly, that is, the physical remains of history. This was surely the case with Mark Lemmon, who returned from the war—already a well-trained architect—to a city for which he was completely prepared. The Dallas of 1919 was fully part of the world because the United States and its soldiers from Texas had enabled America to help its European allies win what was, for everyone, the first global war. As a direct result of the nation's new links with Europe and its position as an equal ally rather

Fig. 5
Third Temple Emanu-el, Dallas, 1917, Hubbell and Greene.

Fig. 6
Thorpe House, Dallas, 1915, Hal Thomson.

than a former colony, American cities were transformed during the 1920s with buildings that had remarkable historicist sophistication and an ease in European quotation. Mark Lemmon had not only learned historicist architectural practice in Boston, but he had experienced historical buildings directly during the war.

Interestingly, but not surprisingly, the study and documentation of post–World War I architectural historicism are not very advanced, even at the beginning of the twenty-first century. This is surely because of the remarkable rise of modernist discourse in the 1920s and the following decade and the subsequent feeling among historians and critics of American architecture after World War II that the winners in the rise of American architecture were the modernists. Therefore, architects who used European historical styles for their university buildings, public schools, homes, and religious buildings were considered retrogressive—analogous to a Darwinian species that had failed to adapt to new conditions and was, thus, fated to obsolescence. So too architects who failed to become "modern." The vast majority of books and exhibitions from the 1930s through the 1980s was defiantly modernist or international, and architects who continued to "civilize" American cities by rooting their plans and façades in the careful study of European prototypes were given plenty of work, but very little critical encouragement. Indeed, architects like Ralph Adams Cram, Cass Gilbert, John Russell Pope, William Welles Bosworth, Bertram Goodhue, Paul Cret, and Horace Trumbauer were lionized by wealthy patrons and important institutions, but scarcely mentioned in the official history of modern architecture then being written by Henry-Russell Hitchcock, Phillip John-

son, Lewis Mumford, Siegfried Gideon, and the young Vincent Scully.

It was not until the last three decades of the twentieth century, particularly due to the impetus of Robert Venturi, whose *Complexity and Contradiction in Architecture* appeared in 1967, that the careful study and documentation of what we might call "historicist modernism" began in earnest. As architectural theorists developed what they called *post-modernism*, architectural historians wrote monographs on the architects whose buildings in various historical styles had long dominated the cityscapes of urban America. Important books on historicist architecture began to appear in virtually every city in the 1980s and 1990s, presenting a clearer picture of American architectural practice in the twentieth century. In spite of this scholarly activity, there has been a real lag in the public perception of American architecture. Most of us in the early twenty-first century continue to believe that modernism was *the* style of American architecture in the twentieth century, no matter the American Institute of Architects urban guidebooks and monographs on historicist architecture that clearly demonstrate otherwise.

This is particularly true of Mark Lemmon's own city of Dallas. His city has been ruthless in its destruction of historically motivated architecture, with whole stretches of downtown Dallas and of the historicist urban core surrounding downtown demolished. When a Dallasite today opens a copy of William McDonald's superbly illustrated *Dallas Rediscovered: A Photographic Chronicle of Urban Expansion, 1870–1925,* the discontinuity between the city in which we now live and the illustrated city evoked in the book is so extreme that there almost seem to be two completely different cities. And this point is made even more clearly when we compare McDonald's book to David Dillon's monograph on modernist Dallas, *Dallas Architecture, 1936–1986*, which begins with the 1936 Centennial Exposition and continues through the building boom of the 1980s. McDonald's city is decidedly Victorian and looks rather like then-contemporary St. Louis, Kansas City, or Denver—anxious to be sophisticated and associated with Europe. Dillon's city looks almost like the realization of a modernist architectural model—gleaming, smooth, perfectly geometric, and grandly planned. The architect who is lost in the shuffle between these two cities is Mark Lemmon, who started his career at the end of McDonald's city and was too historicist to be of much interest to the modernist Dillon.

There is, as yet, no magisterial study of American historicist architecture between the two world wars—the period of Mark Lemmon's architectural maturity—and this book, the first in a series produced by the Meadows Museum, which documents a single architectural career in an emerging American city. It will join the veritable pile of monographs on other architects like Lemmon in other American cities. These books—whether on architects like Houston's John Staub (with whom Lemmon may have roomed when they worked in New York after World War I), Chicago's David Adler, or Florida's Leopold Meizner—have yet to be fully digested. This means that our own understanding of American architecture is hobbled because the dominant, progressive sway of modernism has so triumphed in our history. The architecture of civic memory, in which travel, knowledge, languages, and history inform intelligent contemporary action as much as do technology or reform, has been effectively held back by the ruthless ideological grip of modernism. Architectural civility has been essentially sidelined.

With a solid architectural education in Boston and a tour of duty in Europe, Lemmon became Dallas's first nationally and internationally trained architect. When he came back to the city, he must have felt its urban aspirations. The great urban planner of St. Louis and Kansas City and a participant in the creation of Dallas's own Fair Park, George F. Kessler, had been hired to create Dallas's first comprehensive city plan in 1908, a task completed only in 1911, and the city had worked hard to woo the Methodists to found a university in the city. When it opened in 1915 in two buildings set on a property of more than 600 acres, Southern Methodist University had the largest class to enter a newly formed university since the opening of John D. Rockefeller's University of Chicago. Interestingly, SMU hired the great Boston firm of Shepley, Rutan, and Coolidge (the oldest architectural firm in America) to design its signature building, Dallas Hall (figure 7), the campus's first building, and Mark Lemmon must have felt completely connected to his architectural roots when he saw this thoroughly historicist monument with its allusions both to Thomas Jefferson's library for the University of Virginia and, more remotely, to the Roman architectural past evoked by Bosworth's campus for MIT. The same architectural firm tapped by Chicago to design its museum and public library gave the city of Dallas its first building of national quality and international aspiration.

Before discussing the national architectural parallels between Lemmon's buildings and those of his like-minded colleagues throughout America, it is best to make a distinction between two types of

Fig. 7
Dallas Hall, Southern Methodist
University, Dallas, 1915, Shepley,
Rutan, and Coolidge, Boston.

architecture—the "Moderne" and the "Modern." As the young German and French architects—working under the impetus of Ludwig Mies van der Rohe—Walter Gropius and Le Corbusier were creating a new vocabulary of Modern architecture, another group of architects sought to create a kind of monumental civic architecture called Moderne, or Art Deco, today. Given impetus by the 1925 Exposition des Arts Decoratifs (hence Art Deco) in Paris, this architecture has its roots in various classical and neoclassical modes of architectural expression—replacing the historicist columns, moldings, and pilasters of Greco-Roman classicism with Moderne forms designed to update them. The real catalyst for this type of Moderne architecture was the Viennese architects of the turn of the nineteenth-twentieth centuries who provided their city with a monumental urban architecture free from historicist detail. Moderne buildings are rooted firmly in the architectural past, although this past is reinvented through the application of new forms and technologies. In this way, Moderne buildings are effectively historicist without quoting directly the decorative architectural ornaments of the past. Hence, Moderne buildings fit completely into historicist cityscapes because they are rooted in the study of historical massing and planning. The formality and order of the Moderne can be contrasted in every way with the informality, openness, and asymmetry of the Modern. And, as we shall see in Willis Winters's essay, Mark Lemmon was a very effective master of the Moderne without really ever creating a truly Modern building.

Because Moderne architecture was developed at precisely the same time as the more revolutionary Modern, it was available to historicist architects who could use it as part of their arsenal of available styles, applying the new geometric ornament of Moderne to architectural masses that could equally well have been Georgian, Roman classical, Gothic, or Italian Renaissance. Its use by historicist architects of the 1920s and 1930s was truly national, and Mark Lemmon was certainly open to the forms and materials of Moderne from the late 1920s until his firm closed.

American historicist architects of the first half of the twentieth century built buildings of many types throughout the nation. Yet, it is in the area of religion, civic institutions, and education where their architecture made its most monumental contribution to American urbanism. Indeed, it was rare in the years before World War II for a university, a school board, a religious institution, or a government body to elect to build a Modern building. The Modern was reserved more or less completely for commercial architecture—stores, warehouses, and office buildings. This type of architecture had no direct functional prototypes in European architectural history, and, for reasons both of economy and of scale, American commercial buildings of the twentieth century tended to eschew historicism in their massing and often their architectural ornament.

And even when modernism triumphed in American architecture with the arrival of Gropius at Harvard in 1937 and of Mies van der Rohe in Chicago a little later, many clients for new schools, university buildings, churches, and civic buildings preferred to hire architects whose work evoked a deep historical past. In this way, historicism found its most powerful expression in the architecture of institutions that had deep historical roots, and architects like Mark Lemmon provided buildings with the very latest in structural and technological advances, but with reassuring links to the past. What might be termed the architecture of memory came increasingly to be linked in the minds of modernist theorists and architects to a deep dishonesty. For these men and women, the building of a Jacobethan public school or a Georgian Protestant church was dishonest because it applied to newly conceived institutions the false architectural disguise of the past. And indeed, they were correct. From Ralph Adams Cram and Bertram Goodhue to Mark Lemmon and David Adler, newly carved stone, newly molded stucco, and newly cut wood were applied to completely modern structures of concrete and/or steel in a way that had no precedent in human architectural history. For these modernists, historicist architecture was a sham—an architectural lie—that exposed the weakness of modern civilization by admitting that modern architects were incapable of inventing their own forms for new technologies and new institutions.

The weaknesses of this moralistic argument were not pointed out until architectural modernism had run its course in the last three decades of the twentieth century. Hundreds of architects and theorists began to identify the problems with modernist forms and modernist urbanism, signaling a return to a deeply historicist, knowledge-based architecture. The banality and repetitive formulas of modernist buildings were found wanting in the 1970s and 1980s, and a new architecture of memory—called post-modernism—was developed. This type of historicist architecture, practiced by powerful architects and educators such as Charles Moore (the Piazza d'Italia in New Orleans), Robert Venturi, Robert A.M. Stern, Graham Gund, and Thomas Beebe (who designed the Meadows Museum), based

its ideas less on earlier American architectural historicism than on a vaguely Pop use of varied historical prototypes—both vernacular and "high." Post-modern buildings broke all the architectural rules that had been so primly—and correctly—followed by their historicist predecessors, making it clear that American historicism of the period 1920–1940 was misunderstood as persistently by the post-modernists as it was by the modernists. No wonder we know so little about their work.

Although this publication is intended to document for the first time in published form the architecture of Dallas's most important historicist architect, it is important for all of us to remember that he was neither the only nor the greatest practitioner of this type of architecture in provincial American cities. His buildings were consistently of a very high order—equal in most ways to the best work of his contemporaries in other cities. Yet, when we review his oeuvre in detail, it is clear that he is more important as a major regional practitioner of a national architectural historicism than he is as a sole genius of his own style. For Lemmon, architecture was a civil art—practiced by men (and they were, alas, all men) who had been well trained and who could translate the aspirations of people of power into form. The homes, churches, university buildings, stores, schools, and theaters built by historicist architects for their diverse American clients were not intended by either the architect or the client to be original. Rather, these men sought architecture which was solidly constructed and based on prototypes appropriate to the function—and budget—of the particular building.

For the first time in the history of American architecture, a well-trained architect near a decent library—even in Texas!—had access to hundreds, even thousands, of prototypes for any particular building—making it possible to clothe buildings in period dress and to allow the client to participate in identifying the types of historical allusions evoked by these styles. Churches could be Gothic, Romanesque, Georgian, Spanish Colonial, Roman, or Moderne. And houses had an even greater range. For schools, the architect could use German, Dutch, French, Spanish, and English variants of late Gothic and Renaissance styles—adding a level of geography to history. University buildings too had a great historical range—depending on the historical allusions required by a particular university's history and aims. And, to convince the client of the appropriateness of this or that style, the architect had reference to guidebooks, architectural monographs, illustrated histories, travel photographs, prints, and other visually evocative sources. For the historicist architect, the relationship between real architecture and what has come to be called "paper architecture" was an intimate one, allowing the client to visualize the building without even being able to read plans.

As Willis Winters makes clear in his critical biography of Mark Lemmon, his greatest architectural contributions to Texas were in the areas of educational and religious architecture. Although he built homes, shops, office buildings, country clubs, apartments, and even warehouses, his name would scarcely be known today were it not for his churches, schools, and university buildings. And his preparation for this type of architecture can be placed squarely in Boston/Cambridge in the mid-teens and in Europe during World War I. Because of these two seminal periods, Lemmon was thoroughly grounded in historical architecture—and his frequent Euro-

pean trips later in life are simple proof of the efficacy of his education and military service. His four most important career clients were the Dallas Independent School District, Southern Methodist University, the Port Arthur School District, and the University of Texas at Austin. For these institutions, he built scores of buildings that created an image for public school and university education in Texas that was of national scope and quality.

Lemmon's buildings for the two universities are, in many ways, the least personal of this group of educational buildings. They were not personal, because, in each case, the basic planning principles and stylistic decisions for the campus had already been set when Lemmon took on the task of what might even be defined as campus infill. His buildings for Southern Methodist University were built over four decades and define the campus we see today. Although subservient in terms of their architectural details and materials to Shepley, Rutan, and Coolidge's Dallas Hall, none of Lemmon's buildings copies that building. Nor do they follow a massing plan set by another architect before Lemmon's day. Although less distinguished than the campuses designed for Rice University by Ralph Adams Cram, Columbia University by McKim, Meade, and White, the University of Colorado, or the University of Pittsburgh, the latter both by Charles Z. Klauder, the complex of buildings by Lemmon for SMU has a consistency, a simplicity, and a variety of massing that raise the campus itself to a level that transcends any one of its buildings (plate 2). Unfortunately for Lemmon, who was superbly equipped to teach, no university in Dallas or Fort Worth had ambitions to begin an architecture school during the period of his career, depriving an entire metropolitan area of the

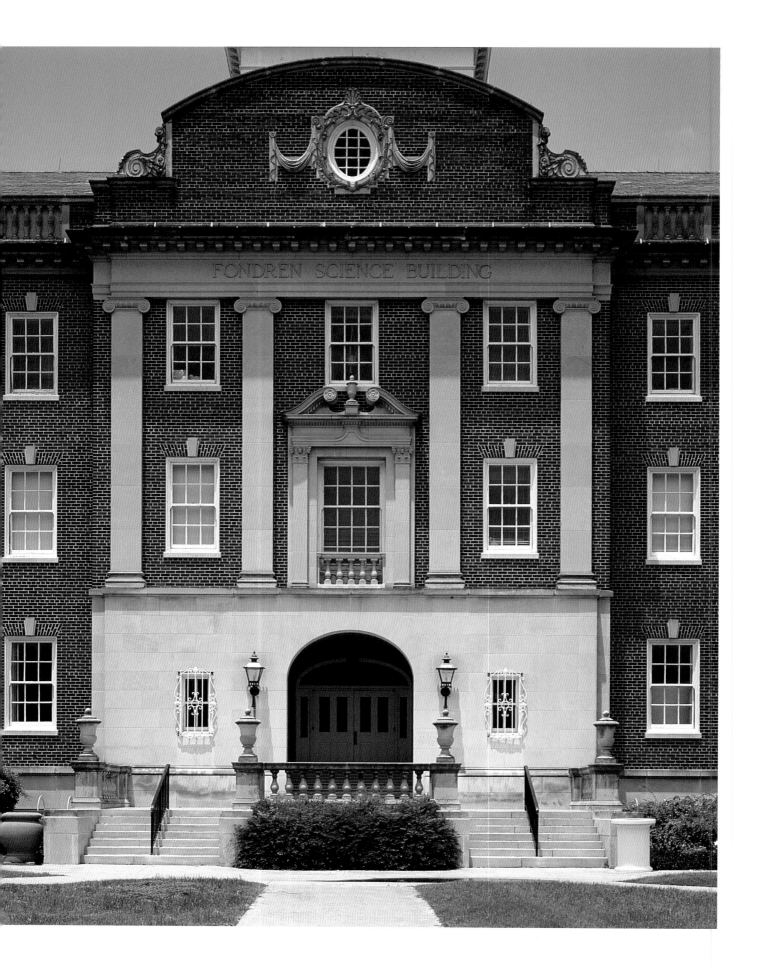

chance to produce its own architectural community —something which it regrets to this day, in spite of the late entrance of the architecture school at UT Arlington.

The task of statewide architectural training was taken on in the Texas of Lemmon's day by the University of Texas (at Austin…then, it was the only one!) and by Rice University, whose architectural school was modeled on those of MIT and the University of Pennsylvania. Interestingly, however, neither of the Texas universities that actually trained architects turned to its own for a campus design, and Lemmon was fortunate to be appointed the official architect of the University of Texas campus in the 1948. While there, he followed the master plan created by his Boston mentor, Cass Gilbert (figure 8, the architecture library), and later by the great French-born Philadelphia architect Paul Cret (figure

Fig. 8
Battle Hall (Architecture Library),
University of Texas, Austin, 1911,
Cass Gilbert, New York.

Fig. 9
Tower Building, University of
Texas, Austin, 1936, Paul Cret,
Philadelphia.

Plate 2
Opposite page: *Fondren Science
Building,* Southern Methodist
University, Dallas, 1946–1950.

9, the Tower building), whom Lemmon knew well as the consulting architect for the Texas Centennial Exposition project begun in 1935. Lemmon's most important buildings for Austin run south from Cret's superb University Library building in a row ending in a spectacular neo-Baroque fountain. Beautifully detailed and finished with materials also used by Cret, Lemmon's buildings are profoundly civil, acting like good guests at a dinner party, who always allow the host the glory.

There is little doubt that Mark Lemmon's greatest contributions to what might be called the historicist architecture of education are his buildings done for the public school boards of Port Arthur and Dallas from the mid-1920s until 1964. This latter group of buildings, both those designed by Lemmon or his firm and those designed under his charge as Chief Architect of the DISD, are the best and most consistent educational buildings ever built in Texas. Built over a period of almost half a century, they define neighborhoods throughout the city and are mostly in use to this day. In styles that vary from Romanesque to Moderne, they are at once solidly built monuments to public education and works of architecture that imbed the education of Dallas public school students in a system of civilized archi-

Fig. 10
East High School, Denver, 1924,
George H. Williamson.

tectural allusions intended to raise the level of our urban culture. In this, they form a collective, if dispersed, urban educational campus that is every bit as good as that of any other city.

Yet, in spite of their quality and consistency, they were neither unique nor pathbreaking. For every quietly assured school building by Lemmon, one can find a score of other similar buildings of an earlier date in another American city. For the purposes of discussion here, I have chosen to illustrate schools in St. Louis, Missouri, and Denver, Colorado, in the teens and early 1920s by a variety of architects whose careers can be linked to that of Lemmon. The four High Schools of Denver, Colorado (East, West, South, and North, rather like Dallas), were all built in the 1920s, and two of them can be related easily to Lemmon's buildings selected for this exhibition. East High School (figure 10) was completed in 1924 and designed in an English Jacobethan style, like that also used by Lemmon, by Colorado architect George H. Williamson. Its three counterparts were each by different architects and each designed in a different style, both to differentiate them from one another and to allude to the various periods of European cultural excellence to which modern Americans aspired. By contrast to the Jacobethan East and the Collegiate Gothic West, South High School (figure 11) looked like a vast southern French Romanesque monastery bordering a park. Designed by the Denver architectural firm of Fisher and Fisher and completed in 1925, it, like the other three high schools of the mid-1920s in Denver, bordered an urban park and landscaped boulevards, lending its historicist grandeur to that of the city itself.

And lest one think that these historicist public schools were developed in the 1920s, it is salutary to

Fig. 11
South High School, Denver, 1925, Fisher and Fisher.

remember that in older American cities, such buildings had been completed well before World War I. St. Louis, for example, a city that Dallas often looked to as a model—particularly after the World's Fair of 1904 transformed its national image—built superb historicist public schools before 1910. The two most important of these are the Dutch/Jacobethan hybrid architecture of the Clark School of 1907 (figure 12) and the sheerly British masterpiece, Soldan High School of 1908 (figure 13), both designed by William B. Ittner. Ittner designed over fifty public schools in St. Louis alone between 1897 and 1914 and many more in twenty-five American states. A future study of the architecture of American public education before World War II will surely recognize the importance of Ittner, whose buildings were known to Mark Lemmon and other national architects through their frequent publication in the national architectural press.

Fig. 12
Clark School, St. Louis, 1907,
William B. Ittner.

Fig. 13
Soldan High School, St. Louis, 1908,
William B. Ittner.

Fig. 14
Marsh Chapel, Boston University, Boston, 1939-1948, Ralph Adams Cram.

If Lemmon was a brilliantly accomplished follower of the best national trends in school architecture, he was equally so when he designed churches. Lemmon was the architect of highly successful churches for various Protestant denominations as well as for Catholic and Jewish congregations. Indeed, few Texas architects could match the sheer range of his ecclesiastical architecture. While Lemmon himself was a Presbyterian, he was deeply knowledgeable about European ecclesiastical architecture and adapted freely from Italian, French, and English traditions. A good deal of the impetus for his religious architecture surely came from his Boston years, when the great Boston architect Ralph Adams Cram built some of his finest churches. Cram's wonderful Gothic Revival chapel and courtyard for Boston University (figure 14) can easily be compared

to Lemmon's later building for the Highland Park Presbyterian Church (plate 3), and Cram's superb Georgian Revival complex for the Ruggles Street Church was under construction while Lemmon was in architecture school. Its handsome spire anticipates several of Lemmon's Georgian Revival spires in later-twentieth-century Dallas.

It is to Ralph Adams Cram, the greatest Boston architect of the first half of the twentieth century, and his various partners, particularly Bertram Goodhue, that one must look for the most important precedents to Lemmon's architectural career in Texas. Mark Lemmon sought to be—and succeeded in becoming—a nationally recognized architect who worked in his own region. For his models, he did not search in Texas itself. One can scarcely imagine the courtly Mark Lemmon on a road trip with David

Williams and O'Neil Ford in the late 1920s photographing vernacular architecture in Central Texas. Instead, his architectural inclinations took him to the established cities of the East Coast and Midwest and to their architectural sources—London, Paris, and Rome. In fact, one of the books in his library, a study in Italian of Italian Romanesque architecture, was purchased by Lemmon on a trip to Venice in 1926. Mark Lemmon knew the cathedrals of northern France, the churches of Georgian London, the rural buildings of Normandy, and the buildings of the Forum Romanum better than he did the nineteenth-century architecture of Central Texas or the missions of San Antonio.

In this way, Lemmon was a nationally ranked professional architect of the very highest standing, and he was known to be impatient with unlicensed and untrained practitioners who worked in Dallas, but who had never attended a professional architectural school of the standing of MIT. Lemmon's architectural and civic personae were very different from those of the best-known Dallas modernists, O'Neil Ford and Howard Meier, whose careers really began a decade later than that of Mark Lemmon and took off only after World War II. Yet, perhaps because of Lemmon's commanding presence in Dallas, the citizens of his city failed to commission important buildings from other national masters of historicist architecture. Unlike Denver, Kansas City, Houston, and St. Louis, Dallas has no buildings by Ralph Adams Cram, Bertram Goodhue (he did, in fact, make plans for a major building for St. Mark's Episcopal Church in 1894, but they were never realized), Cass Gilbert, John Russell Pope, or any

other masters of historicist architecture in interwar America (the only exceptions are the great house built for Count Crespi by the New York masters, Fatio and Traynor, and the Owlsly House by John Scudder Adkins). Indeed, Dallasites experience this type of architecture at its highest level through the buildings of one man—Mark Lemmon—and his various designers and architectural colleagues.

It is, in the end, the sheer civility and solidity of Mark Lemmon's historicist architecture that are so important for Dallas today. Although there have been certain important works demolished to make way for modernist architecture, the vast majority of Lemmon's buildings are still with us . This exhibition and its related publication and educational programs are designed both to document Lemmon's important career and to suggest its place in the larger history of American historicist architecture. In that context, his achievement is considerable, if not commanding. His was not a form-maker's career; he added little to the history of architectural innovation, and it was not his intention to do so. His mentors and progenitors—Ralph Adams Cram, Paul Cret, Cass Gilbert, and the firm of Shepley, Rutan, and Coolidge—all surpassed him as national figures. And even as a regional master of nonregional historicist architecture, he is equaled or exceeded by others with earlier careers of similar scale. Yet, when the larger history of what we might call modern historicist architecture in America is written, it will begin in the years after the Civil War and proceed uninterrupted until well beyond World War II, and the chapter on Texas will be dominated by Mark Lemmon.

Plate 3
*Roof detail from Highland Park
Presbyterian Church*, Dallas, 1937–1941.

THE ARCHITECTURE OF MARK LEMMON

Willis Cecil Winters

Mark Lemmon, Dallas's preeminent historicist architect, died in 1975, at once behind and ahead of his time. By the 1970s the Modern movement had been in command of the American landscape for two and a half decades, and Lemmon, whose architecture was not considered Modern, could easily be viewed as a rearguard figure. Yet Lemmon's work was curiously free of any hard-and-fast rules or stringent ideology; he certainly utilized history, but he exploited it for his own, purely aesthetic ends, casting aside archaeological authenticity in favor of his own freer interpretation. He was an architectural chameleon, effortlessly moving among myriad styles, changing his revivalist mantle from Jacobethan, to Georgian, to Dutch Colonial, and so on. Yet by the time of his death in 1975, when modernist doctrine had given way to post-modern revisionism, Lemmon's work had taken on a renewed relevance. His buildings created a sense of "place" where there was previ-

ously none—from the vast prairies and cotton fields of North Texas to the windswept plains of the Gulf Coast. His architecture manifested a yearning for a different time and a distant place. In Dallas, a city with little appreciable architectural history, Mark Lemmon created it.

Lemmon was born on November 10, 1889, in Gainesville, Texas, the only child of William and Cosette Lipscomb Lemmon. When he was eight months old, the family moved thirty miles east to Sherman—the county seat of Grayson County—where his father taught in the public school system and was later appointed the city's Superintendent of Schools. In Sherman the older Lemmon developed a statewide reputation as a textbook author and was invited to collaborate with several prominent educators in Texas to work on an elementary school text that was published in 1895. Encouraged by the success of this endeavor, Lemmon later formed the Southern Publishing Co. in Dallas to print textbooks

Plate 4
Corner roof detail from Tower Petroleum Building, Dallas, 1929–1931.

written by other regional authors and educators. In 1908 he published a set of elementary school readers for grades one through five, which were adopted and used for many years by local and state school systems across the South. Fortunately, the royalties and income derived from William Lemmon's writing and publishing ventures would serve his family well following his unexpected death in 1909. Although Lemmon died when his son was a freshman in college, he had firmly established the family's name in the highest circles of Texas education—an asset that Mark Lemmon would capitalize on when he began his architectural practice in Dallas thirteen years later.

Mark Lemmon's maternal grandfather was Garland Lipscomb, the General Counsel for the Texas & Pacific Railroad. Lipscomb and his family of six children, including Lemmon's mother Cosette, lived in Marshall, Texas, where the railroad had its regional offices and maintenance shops. Like Sherman, Marshall was a progressive and affluent city, one of the largest in East Texas. After graduating from the State Normal College in Missouri, William Lemmon arrived there to teach at the Masonic Female Institute, where he met his future wife. The couple was soon married, moving first to Gainesville before finally settling in Sherman in 1890. Cosette Lipscomb Lemmon was willingly assimilated into Sherman society, but when her husband died in 1909, she moved to Austin to live near her son, who had entered the University of Texas that year. She would later follow Lemmon to Boston, where he attended architecture school at MIT, and then to Dallas, where he began his architectural career in 1921.

By the turn of the century, Sherman was a flourishing community of 10,000, its prosperity firmly secured with the arrival of the Houston & Texas Central Railroad in 1872. The city boasted a sizable industrial base that included five flour mills, an ironworks, the largest grain elevator north of Dallas, and the largest cottonseed oil mill in the world. Education played a prominent role in Sherman's development as well. Five private colleges ensured the city's reputation as "The Athens of the South."[1] Financial prosperity was further reflected in Sherman's distinguished architectural stock, which doubtlessly made an indelible impression on a young man growing up there. The town square featured an Italianate county courthouse (now demolished), while the nearby county jail, built in 1887, was perhaps an even more impressive civic edifice: a stately Richardsonian Romanesque composition that incorporated the scientifically contrived "rotary" jail into its plan.[2] The city's silk-stocking residential neighborhoods also displayed the affluence of a thriving agriculture-based economy. Luxurious tree-lined avenues that extended north and south from the town square were delineated with extravagant Italianate, Queen Anne, and Classical Revival mansions. These neighborhoods also boasted fine Gothic Revival and Classical Revival churches, many of them completed by the time Mark Lemmon left Sherman to attend college. The city's architectural masterpiece, however, was the 1907 Federal Building and Courthouse (figure 15), designed by James Knox Taylor, the Supervising Architect for the U.S. Treasury Department. Exquisitely clad with dressed and carved limestone and topped by a hipped roof of red clay tile, this Mediterranean Renaissance monument provided an impressionable Mark Lemmon with his first memorable encounter with historicist architecture.

Education, Apprenticeship, and War

Lemmon entered the University of Texas in 1908, graduating with a Bachelor of Arts degree in geology four years later. During his tenure at UT, the original forty-acre campus was a motley collection of stylistically disparate structures, consisting of F. E. Ruffini's Collegiate Gothic "Old Main," and various undistinguished classroom buildings designed by Atlee B. Ayres and others.[3] In 1909 a nationally prominent architect from St. Paul, Minnesota—Cass Gilbert—was commissioned to design a new university library, which was completed the following year, then to prepare a physical plan for the rapidly developing UT campus, an effort that culminated in 1914. Gilbert's library (figure 8, page 13) was a sophisticated and influential building that firmly established Beaux Arts Classicism in Texas.[4] Its form and organization were strongly influenced by McKim, Meade, and White's Boston Public Library of 1892, which was inspired by such classical masterpieces as Sir Christopher Wren's Trinity College Library in Cambridge, England, and Henri Labrouste's Bibliothèque Ste. Géneviève in Paris. This illustrious architectural provenance produced, in Austin, a building of exquisite composition, proportion, and detail. Gilbert's library was also one of the state's first major public structures consciously to reference and engage the Spanish Renaissance style as a pertinent expression of the region's culture and climate. When Mark Lemmon graduated in 1912 and left Austin to pursue an architecture degree at MIT, he undoubtedly took with him his firsthand experience of Cass Gilbert's glorious building, with its luscious limestone walls, rhythmic arched openings, and broad, hipped roof clad with clay tile. The UT Library

Fig. 15
Federal Building and Courthouse,
Sherman, Texas, 1907, James Knox
Taylor, Washington, D.C.

almost certainly would have reminded Lemmon of the Sherman Federal Building from his youth. It is ironic that these two historicist structures, each tremendously important in the development of Lemmon's architectural consciousness, were designed by two prominent American architects—James Knox Taylor and Cass Gilbert—who were previously partners in the same St. Paul architectural practice until its dissolution in 1892.[5]

At MIT Lemmon was exposed to the most rigorous architectural curriculum of any school of architecture in the United States. Still under the indomitable influence of the Ecole des Beaux Arts, the Institute provided students with instruction in architecture that was an integral part of a broader technical program. Illustrious graduates of the Institute included Louis Sullivan, Henry Ives Cobb,

George Shepley, Howard Van Doren Shaw, Welles Bosworth, and two architects whose work Mark Lemmon had previously encountered in Texas: James Knox Taylor and Cass Gilbert.[6] Formalistic discipline at MIT was emphasized through the intensive study and analysis of classical architecture. Lectures on proportion and composition, and courses on freehand drawing, watercolor rendering, and modeling provided students with the practical skills to become solid historicist practitioners. Design theory and architectural history were taught by leading Boston architects, among them Ralph Adams Cram, America's foremost Gothic architect. A course entitled "Building Stones" provided Lemmon and his fellow students with exceptionally valuable knowledge pertaining to the variety and selection of stone masonry used for building and decoration, including its strength and durability, and methods of quarrying and dressing.[7] Without a doubt, the most thrilling experience for an architecture student attending MIT between 1912 and 1916—Lemmon's tenure there—was witnessing firsthand the design and construction of the Institute's new Neoclassical campus on the west bank of the Charles River in Cambridge. Designed by Welles Bosworth, the Maclaurin Building, with its symmetrical wings, broad Ionic colonnades, and low Roman dome, was, upon completion in 1916, widely lauded as one of the most extraordinary examples of monumental Beaux Arts Classicism in America. Mark Lemmon had the opportunity to study architectural design under Edgar I. Williams, one of Bosworth's chief designers. When they graduated from MIT in 1916, Lemmon and his fellow students—among them John Staub, a young man from Tennessee who would later develop a successful and respected practice in Houston—were enthusiastically assimilated into the powerful current of American historicism.

Soon after graduation, Lemmon was hired as an apprentice draftsman by the New York City firm Warren & Wetmore, whose monumental civic edifice, Grand Central Terminal, was completed three years earlier. He worked there for only a short period preceding World War I, but his experience on several of the firm's prestigious hotel commissions—including the Commodore in New York and the Broadmoor in Colorado Springs—provided the aspiring apprentice an opportunity to sharpen his skills under the tutelage of two of New York's most respected historicist architects. Interestingly, during his time in New York Lemmon may have shared a Greenwich Village apartment with John Staub.[8] Although his mother did not make the move from Boston, she undoubtedly continued to provide supplemental financial support so that her son did not have to resort to eating free lunches at bar counters, which Staub frequently was forced to do.[9] While in New York, Lemmon was also able to witness the potent impact of a far-reaching new zoning ordinance that was passed to restrict the height of the city's commercial structures. The 1916 ordinance legislated against the suffocating effect of tall buildings, but left an important loophole that would revolutionize high-rise design in the city: setbacks were allowed above the prescribed cornice line, following the angle of the "sky exposure" plane drawn from the center line of the street.[10] While this ordinance had little application to commercial architecture in a low-density city such as Dallas, it would nevertheless influence the design—fifteen years later—of Mark Lemmon's high-rise masterpiece, the Tower Petroleum Building (plate 5).

Plate 5
Tower Petroleum Building,
Dallas, 1929–1931.

America's entry into World War I in 1917 prematurely ended Lemmon's apprenticeship at Warren & Wetmore. He enlisted in the Seventy-seventh Engineering Division in New York and served as the commanding officer of a supply transport division in France. Like other architect-GIs of his generation, Lemmon was deeply affected by the vernacular architecture he saw throughout the countryside of Normandy and Brittany: picturesque farmhouses, cottages, chateaus, village churches, manoirs, and convents—a visual experience that provided a startling contrast to the standard French Gothic and Romanesque monuments that he studied in college. Following the Armistice, Lemmon and legions of other wartime architects returned to the United States from France with an insatiable interest in French vernacular architecture. Throughout the 1920s, numerous architectural publications and periodicals provided these young designers with the documentary resources sufficient to initiate an eruption of French Eclectic residential design across America.[11] Lemmon's own house on Mockingbird Lane, completed in 1924 and occupied until his death a half-century later, was one of the earliest examples of this phenomenon in Dallas. This resplendent Norman cottage (plate 6) was a salient reminder of Mark Lemmon's military experience in France and of his lifelong reverence for French country architecture.

Upon his return from France, Lemmon—together with his mother, Cosette—moved to Dallas, located fifty miles south of his boyhood home in Sherman. News of the Armistice had previously been greeted in Dallas with wild excitement and patriotic fervor, culminating in the greatest parade in the city's history. The postwar euphoria was widespread, and by 1919 Dallas was experiencing rapid growth in both size and prosperity. Eighty-nine daily passenger trains and 136 daily interurban electric trains passing through the city from as far away as Sherman and Waco made Dallas the leading transportation hub of the Southwest.[12] With a population of 150,000, Dallas was the state's second-largest city, poised for a postwar development boom that would forever transform it from the crowded, rococo center of North Texas agriculture into a modern cosmopolitan city of soaring skyscrapers and far-reaching suburban development. Before the war, Dallas civic leaders—much to the dismay of their counterparts in Houston—had successfully secured the Eleventh District Federal Reserve Bank, assuring Dallas's preeminence as the state's financial and banking capital.[13] This was a defining event in the city's history because by 1919 recently discovered oil fields near Ranger, Burkburnett, and Breckenridge were producing over 63 million barrels of oil per year, and the money was flowing toward Dallas.[14] Bank clearings in 1919 surpassed $1,750,000,000, and this newfound wealth was expressed in the architecture of the city's civic, commercial, and ecclesiastical institutions.[15]

Although Dallas ranked in size as the forty-second-largest city in the United States, in building permits it ranked substantially higher: nineteenth.[16] When Lemmon arrived there in 1919, he was pleasantly surprised to find architecture of exceptional

Plate 6
Opposite page: *Mark Lemmon residence*, Dallas, 1923–1924.

• *26*

Fig. 16
City Hall, Dallas, 1914, C.D. Hill.

quality, much of it designed by Dallas's best firms—his future competitors. Foremost among these was C. D. Hill, whose First Presbyterian Church of 1912 and City Hall of 1914 (figure 16) were among the city's most imposing Classical Revival buildings. In sharp contrast to these two unreserved examples of historicism was the same architect's City Presbyterian Temple of 1915 (now demolished), an extraordinary Norman Gothic cathedral that exhibited the unlikely influence of Otto Wagner and the Viennese School. Hubbell & Greene's Neoclassical Scottish Rite Temple and H. A. Overbeck's Renaissance Revival Criminal Courts and Jail Building—both dating from 1913—were two more examples of monumental downtown buildings that showcased the pervasive historicist tastes of Dallas's architectural community. By no means was historicism limited to Dallas architects, however: several of the city's most prominent landmarks were designed by architects from the Midwest, all of whom assuredly drew upon wide-ranging historical precedents for their projects. Among these were the Adolphus Hotel of 1912 (figure 3, page 4), a splendid Edwardian Baroque masterpiece by the St. Louis firm Barnett, Haynes, & Barnett; the Late Gothic Revival Busch Building of 1913, by the same firm; and the Union Terminal of 1916 (figure 17), a gleaming City Beautiful monument by Jarvis Hunt of Chicago. Only Lang & Witchell, Dallas's largest and most successful architecture firm, dared to stray from the unyielding course of American historicist design. Since 1907, the firm had been producing remarkable

Fig. 17
Union Terminal, Dallas, 1916, Jarvis Hunt, Chicago.

Fig. 18
Southwestern Life Insurance Company Building, Dallas, 1913, Lang and Witchell.

Prairie-style buildings across North Texas, including three notable structures in Dallas: a stunning Sullivanesque skyscraper for the Southwestern Life Insurance Company completed in 1913 (now demolished) (figure 18), and massive Prairie-style warehouse complexes for Sears-Roebuck and the Higginbotham-Bailey Company, both constructed the following year.[17] Despite the appropriateness of the Prairie Style for an emerging architecture rooted in the vast Blackland Prairie of northern Texas, Mark Lemmon eschewed the influence of Frank Lloyd Wright for the comfort and security of the historicist tradition. He was, after all, a rigorously trained classicist whose only wish was to design buildings of refinement and grace, inspired by the great buildings of the past.

When Lemmon began his search for a site to build a house several years after his arrival in Dallas, he selected property on Mockingbird Lane in the predominantly undeveloped township of University Park. On the horizon north of his future home stood Dallas Hall, which was built in 1915 on a windswept field that had been anointed the future campus of Southern Methodist University (figure 19). Lemmon was searching for a phenomenological connection to his Boston architectural roots, and he found it across the prairie in the classical Georgian colossus, Dallas Hall, designed, appropriately enough, by Shepley, Rutan, and Coolidge, one of America's preeminent architectural firms, based in Boston. As he stood on the dust-choked trail known as Mockingbird Lane gazing north toward Dallas Hall, Mark Lemmon began to envision a stately Georgian campus delineated by classically inspired buildings of the highest quality—and the young institution's need for a talented architect to design them.

Between 1919 and 1921, Lemmon worked for Dallas's foremost domestic architect, Hal B. Thomson. Thomson had graduated from UT in 1902 and, following an extensive study tour in Europe, enrolled at MIT, where he received a Master's degree in Architecture in 1907. He opened his architectural practice in Dallas the following year and quickly established a reputation as a designer of suburban houses for élite clients. Thomson was a quiet, introspective man who often developed his designs in seclusion, relying on a handful of talented staff to detail properly the project—under his watchful eye—prior to construction. Lemmon and his fellow draftsmen—among them Marion Fooshee and James Cheek—learned from Thomson the importance of personal reputation, not only as a means of obtaining architectural commissions and repeat patronage, but of securing favorable recommendations for future work as well.[18] While working on prestigious residential commissions on Swiss Avenue and in Highland Park—including Thomson's own house on Potomac Avenue, completed in 1921—Lemmon patiently nurtured the skills he gained as both a student at MIT and an apprentice in New York to successfully execute a design through competent, historically accurate detailing. Lemmon evidently began taking on independent commissions while still working in Thomson's office. His earliest project was a modest Colonial Revival house in Munger Place, built in 1920 for H. Holmes Green, an officer with the W. A. Green Co. Within the year, Lemmon had begun looking for the appropriate opportunity to leave Thomson's beneficial employment and open his own office.

Partnership and Early Success

That opportunity came in late 1920, when Lemmon was approached by F. A. De Witt to form an architectural partnership with his son, Roscoe. The older

Fig. 19
University Park featuring Dallas Hall, Southern Methodist University, Dallas, c. 1918.

De Witt was a native of Massachusetts who came to Dallas in 1883 to manage the schoolbook publishing house Ginn and Company. F. A. De Witt had been acquainted through the publishing business with Lemmon's father and, after his death, had kept a watchful eye on the younger Lemmon's progress through architecture school, military service, and apprenticeship. De Witt's son Roscoe graduated from Dartmouth College in 1914, then received his architecture degree from Harvard in 1917. After the war, Roscoe De Witt returned to Dallas and opened a solo practice for a short while, before joining into partnership with Mark Lemmon in January 1921. Their new office was located in Lang & Witchell's Southwestern Life Building, where the ambitious young architects could survey the burgeoning city eight floors below them, now stretching to the horizon in every direction.[19]

With over forty architectural offices in Dallas in 1921, competition was formidable for a new practice with no appreciable experience or record of completed projects. Eight of these firms were located in the Southwestern Life Building along with De Witt and Lemmon, including Hal Thomson and, in the office next door, an architect named J. A. Pitzinger. Despite these odds the young firm was immediately successful in securing clients and sizable commissions. The first of these would have powerful significance in Mark Lemmon's life. After being awarded the commission for the Stephen F. Austin Elementary School (now demolished) on Washington Avenue by the Dallas Board of Education, Lemmon, accompanied by his mother, visited the home of Trustee George Reynolds to express his deep-felt gratitude. During this social call, Lemmon was introduced to his future wife, Reynolds's daughter

Maybelle. The couple would be married within a year—a felicitous event that elevated the young architect into the upper echelon of Dallas society. To avoid a conflict of interest, George Reynolds resigned from the school board after Lemmon and his daughter were married, and subsequently arranged for the appointment of his close friend Bob Storey to serve in his place.[20] This seemingly inconsequential series of actions would have a prodigious impact on Lemmon's career, not only in subsequent school commissions during his partnership with De Witt, but also in positioning him for lifelong architectural patronage by the Dallas school district.

School commissions—not only in Dallas, but from all over the state—comprised a substantial portion of the work that De Witt and Lemmon would be engaged with over the next five years. Fourteen projects in Dallas, Galveston, Denison, and Cameron allowed the firm to build an impressive educational portfolio that Lemmon, in particular, would be able to capitalize on after the dissolution of his partnership with De Witt in 1926. In order to secure a sizable contract for five new public schools in Galveston, Lemmon shrewdly approached William B. Ittner, a St. Louis architect nationally recognized for his school designs, to form a joint venture. This collaboration allowed Lemmon to work closely with the man who revolutionized school architecture in the United States through the development of the "open plan" concept for school structures. After years of experimentation, Ittner had synthesized his ideas into a science, eventually settling on the E-shaped plan as the ideal layout for his school buildings—a configuration that emphasized light and air within the classrooms and hallways.[21] Ittner's work in Galveston opened

Lemmon's eyes not only to the "scientific" arrangement of a school's functional parts, but also to the splendid variety of historicist styles that could be employed on a building's exterior. Lemmon, whose work up to this point had been mostly limited to either Colonial Revival or Georgian, became attuned to the possibilities offered by Ittner's broader eclectic spectrum, including the Neo-Romanesque, Jacobethan Revival, Spanish Colonial Revival, and Dutch Colonial Revival styles—idioms that he would soon employ with his own school commissions in Dallas and Port Arthur.

Beginning in 1923, the Dallas Board of Education commissioned De Witt and Lemmon for two new high schools that would serve the city's rapidly expanding neighborhoods in west Oak Cliff and east Dallas. For the first of these—Sunset High School, completed in 1925 at a cost of $384,000—Lemmon was rather tentative in his application of Romanesque Revival arches and arcaded masonry corbel tables onto what is essentially a flat Georgian façade (figure 20). The building's front elevation essentially expressed the Ittner-inspired plan within: a central pavilion flanked by three-story classroom

Fig. 20
Sunset High School, Dallas, 1923–1925.

Fig. 21
Goliad Junior High School, Galveston,
1924, with William B. Ittner,
St. Louis.

wings, each terminated by the blank walls of additional wings that completed the plan's "E" configuration. Ittner's Goliad Junior High School in Galveston (figure 21) figured prominently in Lemmon's mind as he undertook the design of Sunset. The high school marked the architect's timid experimentation

Fig. 22
Woodrow Wilson High School,
Dallas, 1925–1929.

Plate 7
Woodrow Wilson High School,
Dallas, 1925–1929.

with historicism, and though the outcome was less than impressive, it was nevertheless a critical step in his evolution as an historicist architect. Lemmon would return to the Romanesque Revival on two more occasions over the next six years, with far more satisfying and acclaimed results.

If Sunset High School successfully reflected the architect's proficiency with Ittner's prototype school plan, it was the 1925 commission for Woodrow Wilson High School (plate 7) in Dallas that presented Lemmon with the opportunity and budget ($548,000) to expand his stylistic repertoire. This time, the architect turned to Jacobethan Revival to create a magisterial façade that encompassed a pair of carved limestone entry arches and flanking columns, quatrefoil panels, quoins, and parapet finials—in a profusion of limestone detail and decoration previously unencountered on any school in the city (figure 22). Through his collaboration with William B. Ittner in Galveston, Lemmon was certainly familiar with that architect's masterpiece, the Jacobethan Revival Soldan High School of 1908 in St. Louis (figure 13, page 16). Lemmon was able to improve on this iconic model, managing to avoid the awkward proportions

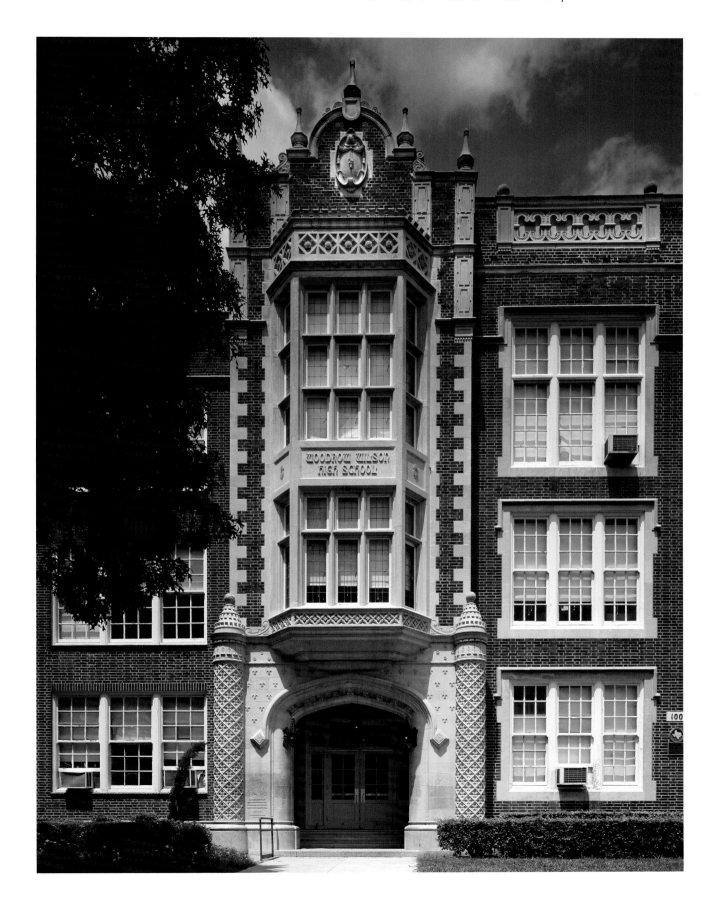

and heavy crown of Ittner's central pavilion. Woodrow Wilson High School marked a significant step forward in the stylistic development of Mark Lemmon. Soon, he would have the opportunity to apply his increasingly sophisticated design sensibilities to other building types.

Lemmon nurtured another major client over the course of his partnership with De Witt. Beginning in 1921, the firm received the first of three commissions from Southern Methodist University—an apartment house for the school's theological department. Although the project was not built, the architects received a second, larger commission two years later for a three-story classroom building housing the University's School of Theology. Kirby Hall, completed in 1924 at a cost of $130,000, was only the fourth permanent structure built by SMU, which had first opened its doors to students in 1915. The University's first president was Dr. Robert S. Hyer, who was recruited from a similar post at Southwestern University in Georgetown to guide the fledgling institution through its difficult early years. Hyer was involved in all phases of the University's formation, but played a particularly active role in the development of an early campus plan, the selection of architects, and the design of the first three buildings. His vision for a tree-lined boulevard terminated by a domed Georgian Revival monument was obviously based upon Jefferson's model at the University of Virginia, and was only partially realized with the completion of Dallas Hall in 1915. Hyer selected the building's architect—Shepley, Rutan, and Coolidge—and worked closely with them throughout the course of design. Fortunately for Lemmon, Hyer was replaced as SMU's President in 1920, so the architect was able to escape his overbearing participation

in the design of Kirby Hall and subsequent commissions.[22] The architect did, however, have to design a building that literally stood in the formidable shadow of Hyer's major achievement, Dallas Hall.

The design of Harper and Annie Kirby Hall (renamed Fred Florence Hall in 1951 when the building was incorporated into the law quadrangle) followed the historicist precedent established by President Hyer and Shepley, Rutan, and Coolidge. To some degree, Kirby Hall (figure 23) references two other important buildings from Lemmon's past: the Federal Building and Courthouse in Sherman (figure 15, page 23) and Cass Gilbert's library at UT (figure 8, page 13). Lemmon incorporated the overall form and proportion of each of these buildings, in addition to the embellished main entrance from Sherman and the row of second-story arched window openings from the UT library. These features were skillfully adapted into the rigid confines of the structure's flat Georgian Revival façade. Kirby Hall was Lemmon's first stylistically successful building as an architect, not only demonstrating his proficiency with the Georgian Revival style but also setting a high standard for future architects at SMU to follow. The project was published by *Architectural Forum* in 1926—two years after its completion—garnering well-deserved attention for De Witt and Lemmon's work. With the completion of Woodrow Wilson High School five years later, Lemmon would further prove his wide-ranging dexterity with historicist styles, placing himself in a position to reap lucrative commissions from enlightened clients throughout Texas.

While Lemmon's office was busy undertaking increasingly larger institutional projects, the architect was also focused on the housing needs of his immediate and extended families. In 1924, he completed

Fig. 23
Kirby Hall, Southern Methodist
University, Dallas, 1923–1924.

Fig. 24
Mark Lemmon residence, Dallas,
1923–1924.

his own residence—a Norman "cottage" on Mockingbird Lane (figure 24 and plate 8), across from the expanding SMU campus—and two years later he built a much larger Norman French mansion for his in-laws on Armstrong Parkway in Highland Park (figure 25). A third house in this same style was also completed in 1926 on South Boulevard for the real estate broker Will Garonzick. All three of these houses demonstrated Lemmon's familiarity with the Norman French style and his fluency with picturesque composition. Lemmon would undertake additional residential commissions throughout his career for friends and clients, the most notable being a Neoclassical estate for William Morris in Preston Hollow, completed in 1937, and a 1939 Highland Park residence for Frank McNeny, a project that demonstrated the curious influence—at least for Lemmon—of Texas Regionalism.

Plate 8
*Living room of Mark Lemmon
residence,* Dallas, 1923–1924.

Fig. 25
George T. Reynolds residence,
Dallas, 1925–1926.

Two final projects dating to Lemmon's partnership with Roscoe De Witt need to be mentioned, both of them bearing the unmistakable influence of two of America's most important architects who were partners in the firm Cram, Goodhue, & Ferguson—Ralph Adams Cram and Bertram Grosvenor Goodhue. The first of these projects was a remarkable competition entry for a new municipal audito-

rium in Dallas. Lemmon's design stood out from those of his competitors as an ambitious Spanish Colonial Revival scheme that balanced simplicity of form against exuberant concentrations of Churrigueresque detail. This style was first introduced by Goodhue in 1915 at the Panama-Pacific Exposition in San Diego and became the dominant mode of regional historicism in the Southwest after World

War I.[23] Lemmon's competition rendering of the auditorium was hypnotizingly exotic, executed with a dramatic interplay of shadows that recalled the work of the New York modernist illustrator Hugh Ferriss, as well as the pen sketches of Goodhue. Goodhue's California State Building at the 1915 Exposition served as Lemmon's specific model.[24]

Along with Woodrow Wilson High School, the final major commission for De Witt and Lemmon before their breakup was a sanctuary and educational building for Highland Park United Methodist Church (figure 26). The site for the church was on the southwest corner of the 130-acre SMU campus—less than a block from Lemmon's recently

Fig. 26
Highland Park United Methodist Church, Dallas, 1925–1927.

completed Norman cottage. Because of the church's proximity to SMU, the congregation desired to express its independence from the university and, as a result, chose to build in the Gothic Revival style. De Witt and Lemmon naturally turned to the work of Ralph Adams Cram, America's preeminent ecclesiastical Gothic architect, for their inspiration. Cram was one of the first architects to experiment freely with French and English Gothic archetypes and to adapt them successfully to the functional, technological, and economic demands of American Protestantism. De Witt and Lemmon followed Cram's lead in their careful composition and placement of the sanctuary and tower and in their competent handling of Perpendicular Gothic detailing. When it was completed in 1927, the church presented a gleaming stylistic alternative to the Georgian architecture of Dallas Hall and provided Mark Lemmon with practical experience with the Gothic, which he would utilize on his first commission in solo practice.

Lemmon withdrew from his partnership with Roscoe De Witt in 1926, a dissolution that was caused, in part, by De Witt's involvement in other business concerns.[25] Although their tenure together was relatively brief, the two architects could look back on their relationship as entirely successful. Working together, they had established good reputations within a short period of time, they had garnered experience with a variety of building types that each would parlay into later commissions, and finally, they had created lasting relationships with long-term clients—particularly Lemmon, with SMU

and the Dallas Board of Education. The two architects were also proud of their work, taking great pains to see that it was properly published—locally, in the 1922 *Yearbook* of the Dallas Architectural Club, and nationally, in the leading architectural journals of the 1920s.[26] In addition to splitting up the remaining projects between them (Lemmon, for example, took Woodrow Wilson High School), they also divided up their small staff. Lemmon was able to entice Frank Kean, a talented architect who had moved to Dallas from Rio de Janeiro in 1923 before joining the firm, to remain with him as they set up a new office in the Construction Industries Building. Kean would play a critical role in the success of Lemmon's practice over the next decade, eventually becoming his partner.

Gilded Cities

For the remainder of the decade Mark Lemmon continued to improve on and expand his stylistic repertoire. His first commission after parting with De Witt also provided him with the opportunity to design once again in the ecclesiastical Gothic style for a Highland Park congregation. In 1926, Lemmon's father-in-law, George Reynolds, presided at the first organizational meeting of the Highland Park Presbyterian Church (plate 9). Lemmon and his wife Maybelle were charter members of the new church, and the architect himself was elected as one of its first elders. Between 1926 and his retirement in 1965, Lemmon would design each component of the

Plate 9
Oppposite page: *Sanctuary, Highland Park Presbyterian Church*, Dallas, 1937–1941.

master plan for the affluent Presbyterian congrega-tion—five structures in all—including the first-phase educational building, which was completed in 1928. Lemmon employed the same materials and vocabu-lary that he utilized at Highland Park United Methodist Church, which was still under construc-tion as the design for Highland Park Presbyterian progressed. Cream-colored brick with stone trim and slate roofs became his favored material palette for Dallas's élite congregations throughout the 1920s and 1930s. Under his historicist umbrella, Lemmon was able to find the right balance between visual sophistication and material economy that appealed to the conservative businessmen who were elders or deacons in these congregations.

In 1927, Lemmon received the largest single commission of his career: the complete implementa-tion of a 1926 bond issue for the Port Arthur Inde-pendent School District. Located on the western shore of Sabine Lake near the Gulf of Mexico, Port Arthur was developed in 1896 as the southern termi-nus of the Kansas City, Pittsburgh, and Gulf Rail-road, providing Kansas City with a vital rail link to the Texas Gulf Coast. This massive undertaking was financed with the aid of Philadelphia capital, supple-mented later with funds raised in Holland. The radial plan of the developing townsite was one of the most unique in Texas, further highlighted by street names such as Wilhelmina, Haarlem, Utrecht, etc., which referenced the influence of the city's Dutch investors. In 1901, oil was discovered only a few miles north of the city in the Spindletop Oil Field, and Port Arthur quickly established itself as the chief shipping point for crude oil, as well as a major refin-ing center.[27] The Eastern oil executives who had descended on the city after oil was discovered in

Spindletop desired first-class public schools for their children, and, beginning in 1922, a series of bond issues was passed by Port Arthur voters to fuel the rapid expansion of the city's school system.[28] Frank McNeny, a Dallas oilman, and both a social acquain-tance and future client of Lemmon's, urged Dr. A. M. MacAfee, a member of the Port Arthur Board of Trustees, to consider the Dallas architect for the commission.[29] Lemmon's impressive historicist port-folio and school experience in Galveston made him the ideal candidate for the job, so beginning in 1927, he and Frank Kean initiated the design of five new schools and four school additions.

The largest of these projects was the Thomas Jefferson High School, located on a four-square-block site close to the Port Arthur waterfront. Lemmon started with a master plan that centered the high school's modified E-shaped configuration to terminate axial-view corridors along each of two perpendicular streets. In an overt reference to the city's early financial backers from Holland, the archi-tect adopted the Dutch Colonial Revival style to create one of the most remarkable façades of any public school built in Texas during the early twenti-eth century (figure 27). The school's main entrance culminated in a tapering checkerboard masonry parapet festooned with terracotta curlicues and finials—an entirely original design that showcased Lemmon's ability to adapt historical detailing freely within a broader revivalist context. For his addition to the Tyrrell School, the architect was even more ambivalent, drawing from a number of sources to create a transitional building that is part-Georgian and part-Spanish, with a featured entrance parapet that somehow references both the Mission Revival and Dutch Colonial Revival styles simultaneously (figure 28). The master of merging historicist styles was Lemmon's Dallas mentor, Hal Thomson, who frequently incorporated both Colonial Revival and Mediterranean sources into his houses. Lemmon was also certainly familiar with William B. Ittner's Clark School of 1907 in St. Louis (figure 12, page 16). The architect continued his work with Port Arthur on four more school projects in the mid-1930s and two final commissions following World War II. The best of these was the Woodrow Wilson Junior High School, completed in 1936 with partial funding

Fig. 27
Thomas Jefferson High School,
Port Arthur, 1927–1929.

Fig. 28
Tyrrell Elementary School, Port Arthur,
1927–1929.

provided by the Public Works Administration. The building's Georgian Revival idiom was typical of numerous schools built throughout the United States in this same style during the PWA era.[30] Lemmon would reutilize the school's formal composition ten years later in his self-referential design for the Fondren Science Building at SMU.

In 1929, Lemmon began work on two projects that would eventually lead to national architectural acclaim and recognition as Dallas's most important historicist architect. Both projects were funneled to Lemmon by his friend Frank McNeny, who was also instrumental in the architect securing the Port Arthur school work. McNeny was a prominent Christian Scientist, and when a new congregation in Oak Lawn decided to build a sanctuary and educational building, he saw to it that Lemmon obtained the commission. The architect triumphantly returned to the Romanesque Revival style for the Third Church of Christ Scientist (plate 10), this time with a generous budget and discerning clients. Here, there would be no hesitation or lack of focus, a problem that marred his first attempt with the style at Sunset High School only four years earlier. The Romanesque Revival provided an alternative for Southwestern audiences to the Spanish Colonial idiom and was more suited in its forms and details to brick construction. While Lemmon and Kean both possessed books on Italian Romanesque architecture, there was little practical precedent for its adoption to meet the requirements of twentieth-century worship, particularly for a modern denomination that had no theological or liturgical roots in Christian history.[31]

Plate 10
*Tower detail from Third Church of
Christ Scientist,* Dallas, 1929–1931.

Fig. 29
Boude Storey Junior High School,
Dallas, 1933.

Lemmon approached the problem in the same manner that he designed the Highland Park United Methodist Church. He saw each church primarily as an issue of picturesque massing, the key to which was finding the right relationship between the auditorium and tower. Only then would he apply the right package of historicist detailing. The architect used the same cream-colored brick as he did at Highland Park United Methodist, trimmed with glorious terracotta columns, pilasters, corbel tables, and lavish ornamentation. The interior of the auditorium was equally compelling. Here, Lemmon created an exotic space defined by a heavy timber ceiling truss and natural light entering through extruded arcades at the two side aisles (plate 26, page 103). Following the completion of this project in 1931, the architect was poised once again to use

the Romanesque Revival on another public school in Dallas. Lemmon's satisfaction with the Third Church of Christ Scientist is evident in his design for the Boude Storey Junior High School in South Oak Cliff (figure 29), where the architect seamlessly adapted the sanctuary façade and its affiliation with what is now a massive square side tower at the school's two-story entrance. Lemmon's enthusiasm for picturesque composition, however, extended to the entire school campus. He expressed the school's functional parts honestly, with only the occasional embellishment, wrapping each discrete element with his standard menu of Romanesque Revival detailing. The architect would successfully use this same compositional methodology—in a modernistic style—on another junior high school before the end of the decade.

Confidence with a New Style

At the time of the commission for the Third Church of Christ Scientist, Mark Lemmon was also working on his first high-rise office building. His client was the Tower Corporation, a development company owned by Frank and Fletcher McNeny. The two brothers were involved in a number of real estate development ventures around Dallas—including the Greenland Hills Realty Company—and were also principals in the Tower Petroleum Company. In 1930, the great East Texas Oil Field was discovered in Rusk and Gregg Counties, 150 miles east of Dallas. The field would eventually become the largest and most prolific oil reservoir in the contiguous United States, and, once again, Dallas was poised to reap the benefits. Dallas became the financial center for the oil and gas industry—not only in Texas, but in Oklahoma and Louisiana as well—due primarily to a favorable policy by the city's two largest banks to accept underground reserves as collateral for financing large-scale production. The resulting influx of oil companies and support services firms—a boom industry that tempered the impact of the Great Depression in Dallas—also caused an acute shortage of office space downtown. The McNeny brothers, recognizing this growing need, commissioned Mark Lemmon to design a "modernistic" office tower on Elm Street, in Dallas's central core.

Although the twenty-two-story Tower Petroleum Building was Mark Lemmon's first experiment with Art Deco, the new style did not represent as difficult a philosophical chasm as he would have originally believed. Henry-Russell Hitchcock observed in 1929

Fig. 30
Tower Petroleum Building, Dallas, 1929–1931.

that a fine line separated Gothic and modernistic skyscraper design, and that the specific character of the ornament was less important than its architectonic function.[32] Lemmon was one of numerous Texas architects who successfully adopted Bertram

Goodhue's and Paul Philippe Cret's abstracted classical idiom into their civic and institutional buildings of the 1930s, but for the Tower Petroleum Building, completed in 1931, the architectural provenance was even more specific (figure 30). In 1922, Eliel

Plate 11
*Corner detail from Tower Petroleum
Building*, Dallas, 1929–1931.

Fig. 31
Second-place entry, Chicago Tribune Tower Competition, 1922,
Eliel Saarinen, Helsinki, Finland.

Saarinen's second-place entry in the Chicago Tribune Tower Competition received widespread coverage in the American architectural press (figure 31). Saarinen's stepped-back massing and vocabulary of ornament, which resembled a modernistic abstraction of Gothic forms, had a profound effect on skyscraper design in the United States. Lemmon further remembered the comprehensive impact that the new 1916 zoning ordinance in New York had on the design of that city's tall commercial buildings. For the Tower Petroleum Building, the architect incorporated the same material palette and coloration that he used in his designs for the two Gothic Revival churches in Highland Park. Carved limestone ornamentation occurs at the building's corners (plate 11), in the window spandrels on the lower floors (plate 29, page 106), as a cap to each vertical masonry pier, and as a continuous decorative band that terminates each of the building's setbacks and attic story (plate 30, page 107). The vertically articulated center section of each façade—bracketed between heavy corners with punched window openings—in particular, owes a heavy debt to Saarinen's Tribune Tower proposal. Throughout the 1930s, Lemmon's dalliance with Art Deco remained in the more conservative Classical Modern vein popularized by Goodhue and Cret. He eschewed the more brazen Zigzag Moderne, with its Mayan motifs, used locally by the Fort Worth architect Wiley G. Clarkson on his Sinclair Building of 1930.

Following the critical success of the Tower Petroleum Building, where he gained confidence with Art Deco, Lemmon continued to experiment with the style on a number of civic, commercial, and institutional commissions throughout the 1930s. Beginning in 1935, he was selected for the design teams of two

Fig. 32
Great Hall, State of Texas Building,
Dallas, 1935–1936, with Texas
Centennial Architects.

Fig. 33
Hall of Heroes, State of Texas Building,
Dallas, 1935–1936, with Texas
Centennial Architects.

exhibit buildings at Fair Park in Dallas, where plans were being made to host the Texas Centennial Exposition in 1936. Lemmon was a member of Texas Centennial Architects, Inc., a consortium of ten Dallas architects working for the Board of Control on the design of the State of Texas Building (now known as the Hall of State). Predictably, the ten firms failed to produce a consensus scheme for the building that was acceptable to the state, so Centennial Architect George Dahl called upon a young Houston designer named Donald Barthelme at the last moment to step in and produce a synthesis of the previous designs and to gain its approval for construction.[34] Lemmon, together with the Dallas architects Ralph Bryan and Anton Korn, were the three members of the original consortium who apparently remained the most active with the project after Barthelme's design was approved.[34] In addition, Lemmon's name is usually credited first in architectural publications from the period (while Donald Barthelme is not mentioned at all), and in his office qualification statements submitted to prospective clients after 1936 and through the 1940s, the architect specifically listed the State of Texas Building's two main public spaces—the Great Hall and the Hall of Heroes—as his work (figures 32 and 33). This seems to confirm the abdication of the building's exterior design to Barthelme, while also suggesting that Lemmon had an active role with the building's interior. Lemmon's brilliance and dexterity as an historicist designer trained in the Ecole des Beaux Arts system at MIT would have certainly prepared him to undertake and produce a Classical Modern interior of such extraordinary grandeur—one of the finest in the Art Deco movement.

Lemmon's second collaborative commission at the Texas Centennial Exposition was for the Museum of Natural History, one of six permanent cultural attractions built by the City of Dallas for the fair. [35] In his master plan for the Centennial, George Dahl created an informal cultural grouping of these structures around a peaceful lagoon, with Lemmon's museum site on its western edge. Due to the project's tight $200,000 budget, the architect was forced to design a monolithic rectangular box conservatively clad in cream-colored Texas limestone (figure 34). The building's two-story lobby space is another exceptional Art Deco interior—well-proportioned with rich materials and details—that supports Lemmon's claim as the principal designer of the State of Texas Building's grand interior spaces.

Lemmon used similar materials and a modernistic program for the six-story Cokesbury Book Store on Main Street in downtown Dallas

Fig. 34
Museum of Natural History, Dallas, 1935–1936, with C. H. Griesenbeck and John Danna.

Fig. 35
Cokesbury Book Store, Dallas, 1936–1937.

(figure 35). Completed in 1937 for the Methodist Publishing House in Nashville, this building reflects the discernible influence of the Beaux Arts–trained architect from Philadelphia, Paul Philippe Cret, who spent the decade of the 1920s simplifying and abstracting the Classical Revival style to achieve a definitive expression of Modern Classicism. By the 1930s the modernistic idiom developed by Cret had assumed its place as the new monumental style for civic and institutional architecture in Texas.[36] Lemmon's later design for the Alex W. Spence Junior High School in east Dallas, completed

Fig. 36
Alex W. Spence Junior High School,
Dallas, 1938–1940.

Fig. 37
U.S. Courthouse, Fort Worth, 1933,
Paul Cret, Philadelphia.

in 1940, is even more compelling in its reference to the style that came to be known as "Cret Moderne" (figure 36 and plate 12). Lemmon was able to study firsthand the U.S. Courthouse in Fort Worth (figure 37), completed by Cret in 1933, and to incorporate its most salient features—including the tripartite entrance and the band of recessed vertical windows—into the school's main façade. The architect also borrowed Cret's distinctive convex window form from the Courthouse to denote the building's main entrance.[37] For the school's functional arrangement, the architect reused the floor plan that he developed seven years earlier for the Boude Storey Junior High School in south Oak Cliff. Lemmon did not engage in architectural plagiarism, however. Paul Cret merely provided the key—not just to Mark Lemmon, but to a generation of American architects—on how to successfully integrate history and modernity into a distinctive new style that was suitably adapted to the demands of a new age.

Plate 12
Corner detail from Alex W. Spence
Junior High School, Dallas, 1938–1940.

Return to Historicism

Lemmon was anything but dogmatic in his adherence to this new style, however. Even more importantly, the vast majority of the architect's conservative institutional clients still demanded architecture that was firmly rooted in history. And so, by the end of the 1930s, while Lemmon was finishing such modernistic projects as the Cokesbury Book Store and the U.S. Post Office in Stephenville (figure 38), he was simultaneously working on a new Georgian Revival addition at the Hockaday School in Dallas, completed in 1939 (now demolished), and his Gothic Revival masterpiece: a sanctuary for the Highland Park Presbyterian Church. Since its found-

ing in 1926 and the completion of the first education building in 1928, Highland Park Presbyterian Church had become one of the fastest-growing Presbyterian congregations in the United States. The second component of Lemmon's master plan for the church comprised a new 1,200-seat sanctuary and education addition, which continued in the Gothic Revival theme of the original building.

The architect once again turned to the work of Bertram Goodhue and Ralph Adams Cram for the overall form and massing of the church, as well as for its details (figure 39 and plate 13).[38] The earliest sketches for the sanctuary indicate a long nave with a square tower positioned at its intersection with the east transept, very similar to Goodhue's disposition of

Fig. 38
U.S. Post Office, Stephenville, Texas, 1936–1937.

Fig. 39
Highland Park Presbyterian Church,
Dallas, 1937–1941.

these elements at his chapel at the University of Chicago, completed in 1928. Lemmon's early scheme illustrates similarities with the main elevation of Goodhue's chapel, including a singular arched entrance portal, a massive Gothic window with tracery, and a pair of miniature towers extending upward from each side of the façade.[39] As the design of the Highland Park sanctuary evolved, Lemmon shifted his ecclesiastical model from Chicago to Pittsburgh,

Plate 13
Window detail from Highland Park
Presbyterian Church, Dallas, 1937–1941.

Fig. 40
First Baptist Church, Pittsburgh, 1912, Cram, Goodhue & Ferguson, New York.

Pittsburgh, the East Liberty Presbyterian Church of 1930–1931 (figure 41), designed by Ralph Adams Cram.[40] If there is a criticism of the Highland Park sanctuary it is in Lemmon's unwillingness to match the sheer verticality of Cram's and Goodhue's Gothic models. Lemmon incorporated tall side aisles at Highland Park, consuming almost two-thirds of the exterior height of the nave walls and leaving only enough space for a row of undersized lancet windows (plate 33, page 114). By comparison, the nave windows at both the First Baptist Church of Pittsburgh and the University Chapel in Chicago are significantly larger and more generously proportioned, and therefore more in keeping with the Gothic ideal. This was a recurrent flaw in Mark Lemmon's Gothic Revival architecture. Later in his career he would have the opportunity to readdress this issue on several other important church commissions.

By the time that he completed the Highland Park Presbyterian Church in 1941, Mark Lemmon had successfully emerged from the Great Depression with a significant portfolio of projects that were produced by a staff numbering as high as fifteen employees (including Lemmon and his partner, Frank Kean). In 1936, Lemmon's office could boast of seventeen different projects in various stages of

where Goodhue's First Baptist Church, completed in 1912, provided the architect with a more "modern" and, therefore, economical version of the Gothic Revival (figure 40). The two sanctuaries share many similarities, among them their basic form and proportion, the conceptual arrangement of architectural elements on the front façade, and, most notably, the graceful lead-coated copper flèche—or spire—that gently springs from the roof at the crossing of the nave and transepts. Yet Lemmon could not entirely endorse Goodhue's spare ornamental program, which was too severe for the architect's traditional historicist tastes. Instead, he utilized a more elaborate system of Gothic detailing and ornamentation that resulted in striking elevations beautifully delineated by light and shadow.

According to Louis Fuertes, an architect who joined Lemmon's office in 1940, the system of stone ornamentation utilized in the Highland Park Presbyterian Church was adapted from another church in

Fig. 41
East Liberty Presbyterian Church,
Pittsburgh, 1931, Ralph Adams
Cram, Boston.

completion—design, construction documents, or construction—with a total value of $2,890,000:

State of Texas Building (Great Hall and Hall of Heroes)	$1,000,000
Base and Exedra for Robert E. Lee Statue at Lee Park	$25,000
Museum of Natural History	$261,000
Fine Arts Building, Texas State College for Women	$147,000
Woodrow Wilson Junior High School, Port Arthur	$589,000
Thomas Jefferson High School P.E. Building, Port Arthur	$105,000
J. E. Langwith Elementary School, Terrell	$84,000
Cokesbury Book Store	$230,000
Florence Nightingale Building, Baylor University Hospital	$128,000
U.S. Post Office, Stephenville	$41,000
Angus Wynne Residence	$80,000
Dr. C. H. Warren Residence	$15,000
Dr. Lee Hudson Residence	$15,000
Dr. P. R. Knickerbocker Residence	$15,000
Fletcher McNeny Residence	$15,000
Frank W. Hall Residence, Georgetown	$15,000
Morton H. Marr Residence Renovation	$2,000

If the average fee for architectural work in 1936 was around 4 percent, then Lemmon took in approximately $120,000, a considerable sum in the mid-1930s. The office completed three final projects immediately prior to America's entry into World War II, including the Joe Perkins Gymnasium at Southern Methodist University, the Frazier Courts Public Housing complex in Dallas (now demolished), and the Air Force Advanced Flying School in San Angelo, an $18,000,000 project that was designed and delivered in twenty-one days. The fact that most of the projects during this period were federally funded portended the evaporation of nongovernmental architecture commissions until after the war. Lemmon was forced to reduce the size of his office in the Tower Petroleum Building, barely managing to keep the doors open in 1943 and 1944, when there were no new commissions at all. The architect's time was expended, instead, on the wartime Renegotiations Board of the Eighth Service Command—a three-person panel appointed to renegotiate unfavorable construction contracts that had been hurriedly let by the War Department. In 1945, Lemmon was elected to the City Council of the Town of Highland Park, a position he held while also serving as a member of the Greater Dallas Planning Council at the invitation of Woodall Rodgers, the Mayor of Dallas (figure 42).

With a prodigious amount of time on his hands, Lemmon could look back on the 1930s as the most artistically successful era of his career. During this period, he mastered three architectural styles—Romanesque Revival, Gothic Revival, and Art Deco—in addition to completing one of Dallas's finest Moderne skyscrapers, and designing one of the most glorious interior spaces in the Art Deco movement. His buildings were immensely popular with clients and the general public as well. In 1940 the *Architectural Record* magazine conducted a poll of prominent Dallas citizens and artists to determine the city's outstanding examples of recent architecture. Lemmon's work placed first (State of Texas Building), second (Cokesbury Book Store), third (Alex W. Spence Junior High School), and sixth (Museum of Natural History) in this popularity survey. In addition, his Florence Nightingale Building at Baylor University Hospital and the Highland Park United Methodist Church both earned honorable mentions. Only one other architect appeared on the list with more than one mention—Lemmon's former partner, Roscoe De Witt.[41]

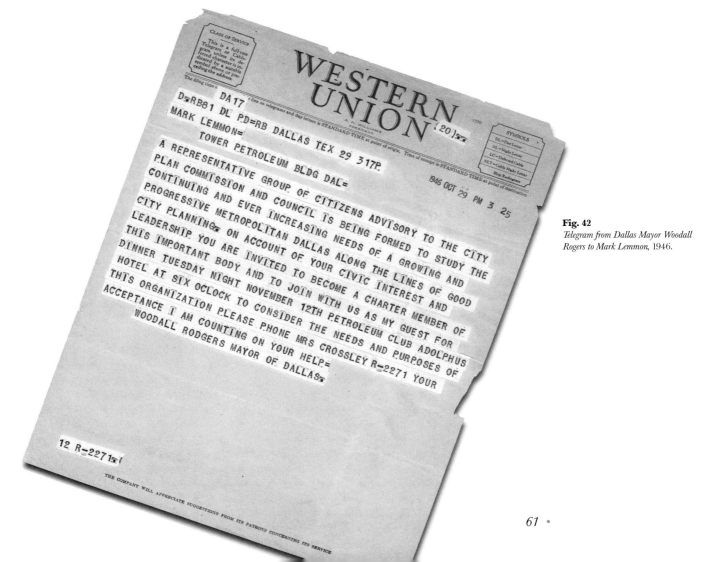

Fig. 42
Telegram from Dallas Mayor Woodall Rogers to Mark Lemmon, 1946.

Transition and Controversy

If the 1930s showcased Mark Lemmon's prodigious talents as a designer of historicist and modernistic architecture, the 1950s manifested the firm's swift transition into a large office replete with work during Dallas's postwar building boom. Lemmon himself was forced to assume more and more administrative duties, gradually relinquishing his cherished design responsibilities to a growing staff of talented architects who had joined the office in the years following the war. Tragedy struck the office in 1951, however, when Lemmon's brother-in-law, George Reynolds, died in an automobile accident while returning from a job meeting in Austin. Reynolds was an accomplished architect who had joined Lemmon's office in 1942, following a five-year career as a sole practitioner. He was responsible for much of the firm's

Georgian Revival buildings, including most of the SMU work, churches in Dallas, Tyler, and Houston, and a hospital in Kilgore. By 1954 the burden of this loss was assuaged somewhat when Mark Lemmon's son, George Reynolds Lemmon, joined with his father and Frank Kean after service in the Navy and after attaining an architecture degree from Rice University (figure 43). Since 1940, Lemmon could count among his most valuable employees the designers Ralph Merrill, George Reynolds, Ard DeFonds, and Louis Fuertes; and senior architects Dabney Lipscomb, Otto Marinick, and Peyton Cooper. In addition, two young architects who would go on to establish successful practices in Dallas began their careers by working briefly in Lemmon's office during this period: W. Overton Shelmire and Harwood K. Smith. By the mid-1950s the Office of Mark Lemmon, Architect, now located in the Thomas Building in downtown Dallas, was one of the largest and most profitable firms in the city, with a core of institutional clients—including the University of Texas System, Southern Methodist University, and the Dallas Independent School District—that any other architect would envy.

Immediately following the war, the office was busy with the second educational building for Highland Park Presbyterian Church and a small commercial structure downtown for Farm & Home Savings and Loan—the final iteration for Lemmon of the "Cret Moderne" style. Lemmon moved his office to this location in 1947, then relocated to the Thomas Building five years later. Also in 1947, SMU, under the leadership of President Umphrey Lee, completed an ambitious campus master plan by Hare and Hare, a prominent landscape architecture and planning firm from Kansas City. Hare and Hare's plan

Fig. 43
Left to right: Mark Lemmon,
Frank Kean, and George Reynolds
Lemmon, c. 1954.

Fig. 44
Lowell House, Harvard University, Cambridge, 1930, Shepley, Rutan, and Coolidge, Boston.

proposed new quadrangles for the Schools of Theology, Science, Business, and Law, in addition to dormitory quadrangles for men and women. Following adoption of this master plan, Lemmon, in his capacity as SMU's Consulting Architect, completed thirteen of the first fourteen buildings during a frenzied period of postwar expansion at the University between 1950 and 1954. The key buildings that would give form and architectural identity to the SMU campus were the Fondren Science Building, completed in 1950; the first seven buildings comprising the Perkins School of Theology, all completed in 1951; the Southwestern Legal Center (now Robert G. Storey Hall), also completed in 1951; and the Joseph Wylie Fincher Memorial Building, completed in 1954. Within a brief four years, Lemmon's office was responsible for the principal buildings that would anchor the University's four main scholastic quadrangles, continuing the Georgian Revival legacy established in 1915 by Shepley, Rutan, and Coolidge's Dallas Hall.

Lemmon seized on this extraordinary opportunity to impose on SMU his vision of the Georgian Revival, which was largely indebted to the twentieth-century Georgian Revival buildings at Harvard University by Shepley, Rutan, and Coolidge and its successor firms (figures 44 and 45), as well as to various Georgian colleges at Yale University

Fig. 45
Eliot House, Harvard University, Cambridge, 1931, Coolidge, Shepley, Bulfinch, and Abbott, Boston.

Fig. 46
Fondren Science Building, Southern
Methodist University, Dallas,
1946–1950.

designed by James Gamble Rogers during the 1930s. Lemmon drew from this selective ensemble of models to synthesize a Georgian Revival context for the SMU campus that reflected his interests in proportion, strength and solidity, monumentality, verticality, and delicate architectural details. His buildings not only established a consistently uniform cornice line and material and color palette, but also introduced to the campus critical architectural elements missing on previous buildings—cupolas, clock towers, and steeples. These essential features of the Georgian Revival style gave definition and char-acter to the campuses at Harvard and Yale and would be successfully used by Lemmon en masse at SMU.[42]

The most significant of these new structures was the $2,250,000 Fondren Science Building, which stretched along the northeast corner of the campus like a great massif (figure 46 and plate 14). Lemmon mitigated the building's inexorable length by frag-menting the façade into three distinct sections of varying heights and setbacks, the central portion of the building being crowned by a tall clock tower with a gilded octagonal dome. The building's relent-lessly undifferentiated window pattern was inter-

Plate 14
Window detail from Fondren Science Building, Southern Methodist University, Dallas, 1946–1950.

Fig. 47
Davenport College, Yale University,
New Haven, 1932, James Gamble
Rogers, Philadelphia.

rupted by a projecting entrance pavilion, where Lemmon compressed the architectural stone detailing for the entire façade into a single monumental gesture. Lemmon was able to overpower and control the spacious quadrangle lying before the Fondren Science Building in the same way that James Gamble Rogers established the urban frontage of York Street at Yale, with his even longer façade for the Davenport College, completed in 1932 (figure 47). Another stylistic device introduced to the SMU campus by this building incorporated end-gable masonry walls that projected above the roofline, terminating in substantial twin "chimneys" —in this case, cleverly concealing the building's laboratory exhaust vents. While there were general architectural sources that Lemmon may have used in his design, most notably Harvard's Mallinckrodt Laboratory of 1927 (figure 48) and Eliot House of

1930–31, both by Coolidge, Shepley, Bulfinch, and Abbott, in many regards, this project was self-referential. The Fondren Science Building owes its largest debt to the architect's Woodrow Wilson Junior High School in Port Arthur, completed thirteen years earlier, in 1937 (figure 49).

The largest group of buildings that Lemmon's office designed was a "campus within a campus"—the $3,500,000 Perkins School of Theology—funded by Joe Perkins, a Wichita Falls oilman. The cluster of seven buildings includes the Bridwell Library and Harper and Annie Kirby Hall, which were symmetrically aligned to define the north and south sides of a courtyard, within which rested the Theology School's centerpiece, Perkins Chapel (figure 50). Lemmon also arrayed two dormitories and two apartment buildings for married students on the west side of the quad, against Hillcrest Road.

This was perhaps Lemmon's finest effort at site planning for the entire SMU campus, reflecting both hierarchy in the disposition of public and private buildings, and coherency in the way that these tightly knit buildings were aligned along two different axes. Lemmon further defined the raised courtyard by a low masonry wall and balustrade, which engaged the corners of four different buildings, along with the rear wall of Perkins Chapel. The front façades of the Bridwell Library and Kirby Hall face each other across this courtyard, and feature projecting porticos with Ionic colonnades, which closely match the chapel's pediment front (figure 71, page 128). As a student at MIT, Mark Lemmon would have studied St. Martin–in–the–Fields, James Gibbs's ecclesiastical masterpiece in London that synthesized the influence of Rome, Wren, and Palladio and provided to the English-speaking world the

Fig. 48
Mallinckrodt Laboratory, Harvard University, Cambridge, 1927, Coolidge, Shepley, Bulfinch, and Abbott, Boston.

Fig. 49
Woodrow Wilson Junior High School, Port Arthur, 1936–1937.

Fig. 50
Perkins Chapel, Southern Methodist
University, Dallas, 1947–1951.

Plate 15
Stairway in Perkins Chapel, Southern
Methodist University, Dallas, 1951.

Fig. 51
Church of Saint Martin-in-the-Fields,
London, 1726, James Gibbs.

Fig. 52
Memorial Church, Harvard University,
Cambridge, 1931, Coolidge, Shepley,
Bulfinch, and Abbott, Boston.

definitive relationship among a classical church's portico, tower, and steeple (figure 51).[43] Lemmon's most immediate prototype for Perkins Chapel was Harvard's Memorial Church of 1931 (figure 52) by Coolidge, Shepley, Bulfinch, and Abbott, which was, itself, a pared-down American translation of Gibbs's St. Martin–in–the–Fields. Lemmon was also simulta-

neously designing a new Georgian Revival sanctuary for the First Presbyterian Church in Tyler—a larger version of Perkins Chapel that was completed in 1949. The chapel's graceful octagonal steeple provided vertical punctuation to the Theology quadrangle, while also working in unison with the cupolas on the neighboring buildings. Lemmon would translate his perfect design for Perkins Chapel into several other Georgian Revival sanctuary projects in the coming years, including St. Luke's Methodist Church in Houston, of 1951 (figure 72, page 130), and Preston Hollow Presbyterian Church in Dallas, of 1962. Another notable sanctuary in Dallas—the Park Cities Baptist Church of 1956 (figure 53)—also owes a strong debt of gratitude to Perkins Chapel. The church was designed by Ralph Merrill, an experienced architect who worked for Mark Lemmon until World War II, before joining with Arthur Thomas after the war to establish the firm Thomas, Jameson, and Merrill. Merrill studied Perkins Chapel closely before completing his design for what would become the grandest Georgian Revival sanctuary in the city.

Two other schools and their quadrangles were also given form by Lemmon's office during the early 1950s. The Law School (figure 54), located in the northwest corner of the campus, received two new buildings in 1951: the Southwestern Legal Center (now Robert G. Storey Hall; figure 55) and Lawyers Inn (now Carr P. Collins Hall). The dominant building of the two was the Legal Center, with an abbreviated H-shaped plan that comprised a lecture auditorium, law library, faculty offices, and seminar rooms. A dentiled cornice line moves around the top of the building, terminating the lower flat-roofed wings on each side of a central pavilion, which has a

Fig. 53
Park Cities Baptist Church, Dallas, 1956, Thomas, Jameson, and Merrill.

Fig. 54
Law School Quadrangle, Southern
Methodist University, Dallas.

Fig. 55
Southwestern Legal Center (Storey Hall),
Southern Methodist University,
Dallas, 1948–1951.

Fig. 56
Joseph Wylie Fincher Memorial Building,
Southern Methodist University, Dallas,
1952–1954.

gabled attic story with masonry end walls and coupled chimneys. The continuous cornice also caps a two-story Ionic portico at the building's entrance. The Southwestern Legal Center was Lemmon's most successful classroom building at SMU. It deviated from the standard rectangular floor plan, which allowed for visual complexity without compromising the Georgian idiom. The Joseph Wylie Fincher Memorial Building, designed to anchor the Business

quadrangle, used a similar plan, and a massing motif like that at the Legal Center, but with different results (figure 56). The flat-roofed flanking wings on each side of the three-story central pavilion appear as minor appendages rather than an integral part of the building's overall composition. The unifying cornice line of the Legal Center is reduced to a horizontal stone stripe in the Fincher Building, which is forced to rely on a half-round portico and matching open-air cupola to establish its architectural dominion over the quadrangle. The designs of the Southwestern Legal Center and the Fincher Building were conducted simultaneously in Lemmon's office, using similar floor plans, yet the two buildings turned out quite differently. The reason can be attributed to Lemmon's abdication of design responsibilities within the growing firm. No longer was the architect able to devote his full attention to every project in the office. Instead, each of these two projects was staffed by a different design team—the Legal Center by George Reynolds and the Fincher Building by Ard DeFonds and Louis Fuertes.

In 1948 Mark Lemmon was appointed Consulting Architect to the University of Texas System, responsible for implementing an ambitious building program at the Austin and Galveston Medical Branch campuses. His duties included advising the UT Board of Regents on the selection of architects for these projects and assuring the conformance of any new structures at the main campus with the development plan created in 1933 by Paul Philippe Cret. During his eight-year tenure as Consulting Architect, Lemmon was responsible for the addition of fourteen new buildings at the campus in Austin; five of these— Batts, Mezes, and Benedict Halls, Townes Hall Law School, and Kinsolving Women's Dormitory—were designed by Lemmon's office. The three classroom buildings proposed for the east side of the South Mall—together with three matching buildings on the west side—were critical components of Cret's campus plan, necessary to frame the lawn behind the Littlefield Fountain and to focus attention on the architect's seventeen-story library tower behind the Main Building. Cret also saw these buildings as essential in mitigating the steep grade between Twenty-first

Street and the plaza in front of the Main Building.[45] The architect designed the first of the six classroom buildings on the west side of the mall, in what has been described as the "University of Texas" style—a blend of architectural features, materials, and details taken from the Spanish Renaissance buildings built in 1933 as the first installment of the development plan. Cret's Music Building of 1942 featured a wide red tile roof, Texas limestone and shellstone walls, a third story under the overhanging roof eave with wider window openings, and prominent entries accented by lavish ornamentation and a second-floor balcony railing.[45] Lemmon slavishly adhered to this strict architectural formula developed by Cret in his design of Batts, Mezes, and Benedict Halls, which were essentially three identical buildings with recessed courtyards between them (figure 73, page 131, and figure 74, page 132). Lemmon was not interested in innovation, nor was he intent on making a personal statement with the commission. He simply desired that these three classroom structures conform with the predominant architectural character of the campus, and Cret's Music Building across the mall provided him with the best model to follow.

After the designs for the South Mall buildings as well as those for the Pharmacy and Journalism buildings were published in late 1949, students at the UT School of Architecture, under the growing influence of the Bauhaus and European modernism, vehemently protested the blatant historicism by Lemmon and his associate architects. In a letter submitted to the architects and the University's faculty building committee, the students wrote:

The dummy dormers, ornate friezes and super-imposed pediments will waste the cost of much additional equipment; their exterior decoration probably will rely on extravagant applied ornamentation, rather than on the simple beauty of materials; their room arrangement pays more attention to the preservation of a symmetrical axis, than to the requirements for adequate daylight, noise isolation, easy traffic circulation and minimum square footage, and they are not what they are supposed to be—economical and efficient university buildings.[46]

The students went on to complain, "If the university is to fulfill its role in developing the cultural background of the coming generation, its entire attitude should be creative, not imitative." The students also cited recent buildings at other universities, including MIT and Harvard, which they lauded for "beginning to build in a free, rational and contemporary feeling."[47] One of the first campus buildings in the United States to be built in the new International Style was the Harvard Graduate Center, a sprawling complex of dormitories and communal facilities designed by Walter Gropius and the Architects Collaborative in 1949.[48] Lemmon traveled to Harvard with his friend Dudley K. Woodward, Chairman of the UT Board of Regents, to inspect this new architecture. He interviewed a librarian in a nearby Georgian building who referred to Gropius's Graduate Center as "a modern bottling plant."[49] Lemmon returned to Texas and defended his role as Consulting Architect, as being charged by the Board of Regents to implement Cret's campus plan, including the adopted historicist style. He was quoted by *The Dallas Morning News* as saying, "I think it [Cret's plan] is lovely and most people agree."[50] Lynn Landrum, writing for the *Morning News,* dedi-

cated several columns to the issue in November 1949. After presenting the case of the students, together with Lemmon's lame response, she finally weighed in with her own opinion. She wrote:

> Great architecture, young gentlemen, is often old because it has to be great to be allowed to survive after others, which were only free, rational and contemporary [i.e., modern buildings], are torn down. Mr. Lemmon gets the decision.[51]

Although he won this battle in the court of public opinion, Mark Lemmon was shaken to his innermost core. Never before had anyone questioned his philosophy or his stature as one of the leading historicist architects in the state. The crisis of style, which had afflicted countless American architects after the war, had descended upon him with a vengeance. In the coming years, he would gradually turn away from historicism and convert to the functionalist philosophy of Gropius, Neutra, and the other European modernists who had emigrated to the United States before and after the war. With few exceptions (SMU and UT Austin), he was forced to abandon his Beaux Arts training and his long-standing architectural sources—Cram, Goodhue, and Cret. Although he would occasionally return to historicism for ecclesiastical commissions, including churches in Houston, Dallas, Rosenberg, Midland and San Angelo, his two best church projects, completed near the end of his career, were both modern. Lemmon's swift assimilation of modernism coincided with the dramatic postwar expansion of the Dallas school system, a program under his direct control as the School Board's Consulting Architect.

Modernism

In 1947 the old Board of Education was replaced by the City of Dallas with an independent taxing agency and an elected school board. Mark Lemmon, who had previously served the School Board as Consulting Architect, was appointed to the same position by the new school district's Board of Trustees. Until his retirement in 1968, Lemmon would direct an ambitious $250,000,000 building campaign that would place new or expanded school facilities in virtually every neighborhood in the city. As Consulting Architect to the DISD for twenty-one years, Lemmon enjoyed perhaps the most powerful public role that an architect ever possessed in Dallas. He was responsible for recommending to the Board the selection of architects for each project and also for bringing their plans forward for approval prior to bidding and construction. In this capacity, he strongly influenced the design of all new public schools in Dallas for over two decades. As a recent convert to modernism following the UT controversy, Lemmon was intent on administering a building program that responded to the educational needs of mid-century America through new functional arrangements, new technologies, and new materials. Lemmon certainly recalled his experience in Galveston with William B. Ittner's "scientific" school floor plans that emphasized natural light and air circulation—objectives that were still valid forty years later. Beginning in the late 1940s modern schools were being published by architectural periodicals, providing Dallas architects with compelling glimpses of contemporary design by such architects as John Carl Warnecke, Ernest J. Kump, and Mario J. Ciampi in California; Perkins & Will in the Midwest; Curtis & Davis in Louisiana;

Fig. 57
Casa View Elementary School,
Dallas, 1951–1953.

Fig. 58
W.W. Samuell High School, Dallas,
1954–1957.

and Arthur Gould Odell in North Carolina. Texas could also boast of several outstanding new schools: The St. Rose of Lima School in Houston by Donald Barthelme and the Central Elementary School in Texarkana by George Dahl, completed in 1948 and 1949, respectively, were among the state's earliest notable schools designed in the modern idiom. The finest modern schools in the Southwest, however, were designed throughout the 1950s by the Houston firm Caudill, Rowlett, Scott, and Associates. The firm's Norman High School in Norman, Oklahoma, San Jacinto Elementary School in Liberty, and San Angelo Central High School were functionally and technologically innovative, and strikingly modern.[52]

Between 1945 and 1954, the Board of Education and DISD successfully passed between them four bond referendums totaling $86,330,000, funding 105 new schools or school additions.[53] During this period Lemmon allocated to his own office eight new elementary schools and one new high school—by far the most commissions that any single firm in Dallas received. The best of these new schools were the Casa View Elementary School of 1953 (figure 57), the Albert Sydney Johnston Elementary School of 1956, and the W. W. Samuell High School in Pleasant Grove, completed in 1957 (figure 58 and plate 16). Ard DeFonds was Lemmon's designer who was responsible for much of this work. By the

Plate 16
Detail of W.W. Samuell High School,
Dallas, 1954–1957.

mid-1950s Lemmon and his staff had worked out a standard recipe for the design of each school, and Lemmon himself began insisting upon this strict modernist doctrine with the city's architects. Already disturbed that Lemmon was taking a 7/8 percent fee out of their typical 6 percent fee, and chafing at the power he wielded as the district's Consulting Architect, firms and offices throughout the city were poised to launch a virulent campaign against him.

The spark was provided in February 1955, when the President of the School Board contacted two Dallas architects to discuss the possible duplication of school plans in an attempt to save the district money. The response came in the form of a nineteen-page report prepared by the Dallas chapter of the American Institute of Architects that heavily criticized the Board for its consideration of standardized school plans and demanded the elimination of the office of Consulting Architect. The architects claimed that Lemmon's average annual fee of $80,000 was three times the salary of a full-time administrator who could oversee design and construction for the school district. The architects also petitioned the Board for relief from "obsolete design requirements relating to construction methods, materials and exterior design."[54] Lemmon was staggered by the ferocity of this attack, especially considering that the petitioners included his former partner, Roscoe De Witt, serving as the AIA President, and a former employee, Harwood K. Smith. He quietly issued a one-page response to the architects' charges, defending his record as Consulting Architect—not only for DISD, but for Southern Methodist University and the University of Texas as well—and denying their assertion that under his supervision, schools in Dallas had cost more than

schools elsewhere in the country. After a series of editorials in *The Dallas Times Herald,* including one that called for an independent investigation of the AIA's claims, the School Board issued a policy statement concerning the construction of school buildings that defended the district's right to consider the use of plans for duplicate schools, defended the position of the Consulting Architect, and expressed surprise over the architects' claim that they were forced to use obsolete designs. In June, the School Board formally rejected the *Times Herald's* offer to pay for an outside impartial investigation, and then, later in the month, approved the use of a duplicate plan from Thomas Jefferson High School for a new high school in east Dallas. The architects were defeated, and Mark Lemmon would continue in his role as Consulting Architect, guiding the design of Dallas's public schools through his strict modernist regimen for eleven more years.

While the controversy with DISD was still raging, two important projects in Lemmon's office—both designed by Ard DeFonds—were nearing completion. In 1948, the UT Board of Regents voted to assume control of the Southwestern Medical College in Dallas, a small school privately operated by the Southwestern Medical Foundation. The new school would be the northern branch of the University of Texas Medical School and would receive an infusion of state funds to initiate a building program at the school's shantytown campus located on Harry Hines Boulevard. Lemmon was the logical choice as the architect of the school's first permanent structure, the Cary Basic Sciences Building (figure 59), which was completed in 1955. The architect began work immediately on the second phase of the Southwestern Medical College, the nine-story Hoblitzelle Clinical

Sciences Building, a brick and glass structure that was the second-tallest building of Lemmon's career and his first large-scale investigation of a glass curtain wall. Also in 1955, construction was completed on a five-story addition to Dallas's City Hall—a 1914 Beaux Arts monument designed by C. D. Hill (figure 16, page 28). Lemmon was appointed Consulting Architect and was responsible for the building's design. His associate architect on the project was one of his inquisitors in the DISD fiasco—Harwood K. Smith.

With his design for the municipal annex and other projects from this era, a style began to emerge in Lemmon's architecture that defined his—at times, banal—modernist discourse. His modern buildings were mostly of brick construction with horizontal strip windows or larger expanses of glass defined by a heavy molding or trim. This was a common trait of his DISD and Southwestern Medical College work, and also characterized several other projects—a small downtown office building for Lone Star Gas, the Municipal Building Annex, and the Kinsolving Hall Dormitory at UT, which was completed in 1958. The architect and his staff of designers were strong at functional massing—i.e., expressing the different functions of the building through the efficient organization of the floor plan—but they typically produced uninspired elevations that were devoid of modernist content and technology. The exception to this was the Hoblitzelle Clinical Sciences Building, but even here the seven-story expanse of curtain wall was encased within a masonry frame (figure 59).

By the 1950s Dallas was experiencing explosive growth, which was reflected in the wholesale modernist makeover of the city's downtown. Old buildings were reskinned with aluminum panels, and new towers and mixed-use complexes were on the drawing boards. The two best public buildings from this era were both designed by George Dahl, another nemesis of Lemmon's from the DISD affair. Dahl's buildings—the Dallas Public Library of 1953 and the Dallas Convention Center of 1957—were vastly superior to Lemmon's later addition to the Dallas City Hall. While the City of Dallas utilized local architects for its public projects downtown, the best these architects could hope for from the private commercial sector was to be teamed with an out-of-town firm as its associate. Gill & Harrell, for example, were the associate architects on downtown's first major postwar project—the thirty-six-story Republic National Bank designed by Harrison & Abramovitz of New York. Mark Lemmon was appointed associate architect on the Southland Center, a sizable mixed-use project completed in 1958 that comprised the tallest office tower west of the Mississippi and a six-hundred-room Sheraton Hotel. The architect for the project was Welton Becket of Los Angeles. Lemmon was also the associate architect on another large project completed in 1958—a massive Operations Center at Love Field for Braniff Airlines. In his role as associate architect on these two projects, Lemmon had no design responsibilities; he acted as the liaison between the Dallas client and the architect-of-record and was also responsible for supervising construction. The final architectural association of Lemmon's career was with his old friend, George Dahl, who was forced to team up with him by the General Services Administration on a new Federal Courthouse and Office Building downtown. The two architects maintained a shared office throughout the project, each contributing staff as the need

Fig. 59
Cary Basic Sciences Building (foreground)
and *Hoblitzelle Clinical Sciences Building,*
Southwestern Medical College,
Dallas, 1952–1958.

arose. The personal acrimony between the two was manifested in the lackluster architecture of the building when it was completed in 1963.

Four Late Churches

Toward the end of his career, Lemmon was once again involved with ecclesiastical commissions throughout the state. Two of these were modern church campuses for new clients in Wichita Falls and Galveston, and two were historicist additions to existing campuses designed by Lemmon in Dallas. The First Presbyterian Church in Wichita Falls, completed in 1962, and the Moody Memorial Methodist Church in Galveston, completed in 1964, were two of the architect's most successful modernist buildings. Both churches were built on featureless, flat sites and incorporated similar planning attributes

concerning the functional arrangement of the sanctuary, chapel, educational wings, and courtyard. The First Presbyterian Church (figure 60), with its starkly contemporary bell tower, is a highly distilled modernist adaptation of De Witt and Lemmon's Highland Park United Methodist Church of 1927 (figure 26, page 41). The Moody Memorial Methodist Church in Galveston (figure 61), with its cathedral-like proportions and slender flèche crowning its tall roof, is a modernist rendition of the architect's Highland Park Presbyterian Church sanctuary of 1941 (figure 39, page 57). While it is interesting to speculate whether Lemmon was consciously trying to

Fig. 60
First Presbyterian Church,
Wichita Falls, 1956–1962.

Fig. 61
Moody Memorial Methodist Church,
Galveston, 1961–1964.

bring closure to his career by reinterpreting his Gothic Revival masterpieces in a modernist idiom, it should also be noted that the architect was simultaneously working on additions to the very churches he was emulating. Thus, Dallas's preeminent historicist architect closed his career with additions in his beloved Gothic Revival style for two Highland Park congregations that had provided him with loyal patronage since the 1920s.

Mark Lemmon retired from architecture in 1968, but his office in the Southland Center had been greatly downsized and become very quiet over the previous three years. He kept the office open at the request of DISD Superintendent Dr. W. T. White, who persuaded the sixty-six-year-old architect to maintain his indispensable role as the district's Consulting Architect for a little longer. He had much time to reflect on his illustrious career, including the sixty-one public schools his office designed in eleven Texas cities, or the university campuses that he helped shape—including the one across Mockingbird Lane from the Norman cottage he built in 1924. Perhaps he recalled the dozens of church projects throughout the state that his office had designed, including his own church, of which he was a founding member and for which he was responsible for five separate buildings over a span of thirty-seven years. As he traveled throughout his beloved France with his wife, Maybelle, he was in the presence once again of the cottages and buildings of his younger years that had inspired him to introduce French Norman architecture to his adopted home in Texas. The recollection of his exquisite work provided the old architect with much-deserved solace in the turbulent world of the late 1960s and early 1970s. The business of architecture had grown complicated,

and the old ways of managing a practice had become obsolete.

By 1975, Mark Lemmon was suffering from a slow, irregular heartbeat. His eyesight was failing him, but he could still clearly imagine the glorious works from throughout his career—Woodrow Wilson High School, Thomas Jefferson High School in Port Arthur, Third Church of Christ Scientist, Tower Petroleum Building, Boude Storey Junior High School, the Great Hall in the State of Texas Building at the Centennial Exposition, Cokesbury Book Store, Highland Park Presbyterian Church sanctuary, Alex W. Spence Junior High School, Fondren Science Building, Perkins Chapel, the South Mall buildings at the University of Texas, W. W. Samuell High School, Hoblitzelle Clinical Sciences Building, and Moody Memorial Methodist Church in Galveston. Few architects could boast of such a distinguished and memorable list of projects. Maybelle had arranged for nurses around the clock to care for him, and although he was able to stand and dress each day, he spent most of his time in a wheelchair. On Sunday, December 21, 1975, after watching the Dallas Cowboys play the New York Jets on television, Lemmon began to complain of discomfort. He was taken to the hospital, where he passed away the next day, December 22, of an acute aneurysm. Lemmon's funeral was held on Christmas Eve in the sanctuary of Highland Park Presbyterian Church. The Senior Minister, Dr. B. Clayton Bell, conducted the service, which was brightened by performances of Haydn and Mozart by the Dallas String Quartette. Then the Pastor Emeritus of the church, Dr. William M. Elliott—Lemmon's friend and client for many years—gave the oration. After recounting the architect's achievements and direct-

Plate 17
*Sanctuary, Highland Park Presbyterian
Church*, Dallas, 1937–1941.

ing the gaze of the congregants around his splendid Gothic Revival interior (plate 17), Dr. Elliott remarked, ". . . this sanctuary is not only a temple of God, but also a monument to Mark Lemmon."

Legacy

A Dallas resident who looks around the city, particularly one who knows where to look, will be surprised at how great an imprint Mark Lemmon left behind. At the same time, it is astonishing to consider how long the eclipse of his reputation has lasted. Yet Lemmon's physical presence is all around—over ninety extant buildings and projects in Dallas alone—structures that bear articulate testimony to the city's dramatic transformation into a bustling cosmopolitan center during the 1920s and 1930s. Lemmon's reputation seems to have suffered, in part, because he projected no distinct personal style. With the exception of his cherished Gothic Revival–the style with which he was most closely associated–the architect's robust architectural vocabulary did not overtly express his personality, except, perhaps, in his indefatigable devotion to integrity and high standards.

Mark Lemmon was not an innovator. He admired the work of Bertram Grosvenor Goodhue, one of America's most brilliant and original architects until his death in 1924. Lemmon's Beaux Arts-influenced philosophy was closely aligned with that of the great eclectic architects on the east coast, in particular, Cass Gilbert and Paul Philippe Cret. Each of these men practiced during an era when architecture was changing radically from out-moded historicist principles to the precepts of the Modern movement. Lemmon himself was caught in the middle of this

stylistic dilemma when he incorporated Cret-influenced classicism into the design of his classroom buildings at the University of Texas. Mark Lemmon was too genteel, too chivalrous, to participate publicly in this debate. Instead, his buildings—whatever their style—expressed his architectural convictions in an irrefutable manner. Although he successfully adapted to the Art Deco style during the 1930s, designing some of the city's greatest Moderne buildings during this period, the architect failed to make a completely successful transition to modernism, with its machine-like vocabulary devoid of ornamentation.

Looking back over the first half of the twentieth century, one can see that Mark Lemmon's oeuvre is matched only by a small handful of architects and firms practicing in Dallas during this period. Among these, C.D. Hill & Co. and Herbert M. Greene primarily employed the Classical Revival style in such institutional monuments as the First Presbyterian Church, the Scottish Rite Cathedral and the Municipal Building, all built between 1912 and 1914. Both of these architects had retired by 1930, although Greene's principal partner, George Dahl, later continued the firm under his own name well into the 1970s. Dahl and Lemmon became fierce competitors, operating the two most successful offices in Dallas after World War II. Dahl, an extraordinarily gifted architect responsible for the planning and design of the Texas Centennial Exposition in 1936, was more successful than Lemmon in navigating his way into the modern world of architectural business: his firm was the first in Dallas to export architecture beyond the state's boundaries and the first to adapt modernism to a large-scale commercial practice. Dahl and Lemmon collaborated late in their careers on a prestigious new federal courthouse in downtown Dallas, although it was a bittersweet association with dreadful results.

Only the firm of Lang & Witchell displayed the stylistic breadth remotely close to the dimension of that of Mark Lemmon. Like Lemmon's, the firm was well versed in the Gothic Revival and in 1931 completed two elegant Moderne office buildings downtown for the Dallas Gas Co. and Dallas Power & Light. In 1913 and 1914, Lang & Witchell also introduced the Prairie Style to Dallas in a residence and warehouse for Rufus Higginbotham. Lemmon, by contrast, would have no part of the Prairie School movement, despite its distinguished pedigree as a purely American phenomenon. Neither did Lemmon

accede to the widespread influence of the Spanish and Mediterranean revivals, two vastly popular residential styles prevalent in Dallas between the world wars. Instead, the architect focused on the architectural styles that he was most familiar with and had experienced first-hand during his education and apprenticeship in Boston and New York, as well as his military service in France. Given the extraordinary diversity of his repertoire, which encompassed Georgian, Romanesque, Jacobethan, Gothic, French Norman, and Dutch Colonial, and the magisterial buildings that he built in each of these styles, Mark Lemmon's stature as Dallas's foremost historicist architect is secure.

1. Brian Hart, "Sherman, Texas," in *The Handbook of Texas Online* (http://www.tsha.utexas.edu/handbook/online/articles/view/SS/hds3.html, accessed October 24, 2002).

2. Willard B. Robinson, *The People's Architecture: Texas Courthouses, Jails, and Municipal Buildings* (Austin: Texas State Historical Association, 1983), pp. 88–90.

3. Roxanne Kuter Williamson, "A History of the Campus and Buildings of the University of Texas with Emphasis on the Sources for the Architectural Styles" (Master's thesis, University of Texas at Austin, 1965), pp. 2–6.

4. Lawrence W. Speck, *Landmarks of Texas Architecture* (Austin: University of Texas Press, 1986), p. 55.

5. Roxanne Kuter Williamson, *American Architects and the Mechanics of Fame* (Austin: University of Texas Press, 1991), p. 71.

6. Ibid., p. 164.

7. "Massachusetts Institute of Technology Department of Architecture Course of Instruction," *Architectural Record* (Date not known): pp. 443–52.

8. Interview with Louise Fuertes, January 8, 1980.

9. Howard Barnstone, *The Architecture of John Staub: Houston and the South* (Austin: University of Texas Press, 1979), p. 3.

10. Robert A. M. Stern, Gregory Gilmartin, and Thomas Mellins, *New York 1930: Architecture and Urbanism between the Two World Wars* (New York: Rizzoli International Publications, Inc., 1987), p. 508.

11. See, for example, William D. Foster, *Cottages, Manors, and Other Minor Buildings of Normandy and Brittany* (New York: Architectural Book Publishing Company, 1926), a book in Mark Lemmon's personal library. Another prominent Dallas architect, George Leighton Dahl, photographed and authored *Portals, Doorways, and Windows of France* (New York: Architectural Book Publishing Company, 1925) following his wartime service in Europe. The idiosyncratic Dallas architect Charles Dilbeck, who designed numerous French Eclectic cottages and estates, possessed in his private library Raymond Quenedey's *La Normandie: Recueil de Documents d'Architecture Civile* (Paris: F. Contet, Editeur d'Art, 1927).

12. Ellis A. Davis and Edwin H. Grobe, eds., *The Encyclopedia of Texas* (Dallas: Texas Development Bureau, n.d.), p. 48.

13. Maxine Holmes and Gerald D. Saxson, eds., *The WPA Dallas Guide and History* (Denton: University of North Texas Press, 1992), pp. 87–89.

14. Davis and Grobe, *The Encyclopedia of Texas*, p. 26. By comparison, production in the great Spindle Top and Sour Lake fields in southeast Texas had dwindled to a little over 3 million barrels per year by 1919.

15. Ibid, p. 47.

16. Ibid.

17. For a comprehensive selection and discussion of Dallas architecture during this period, see William L. McDonald, *Dallas Rediscovered: A Photographic Chronicle of Urban Expansion, 1870–1925* (Dallas: Dallas Historical Society, 1978), and Larry Paul Fuller, ed., *The American Institute of Architects Guide to Dallas Architecture* (Dallas: Dallas Chapter, American Institute of Architects, 1999).

18. David Hurlbut, "Designer of Dreams: Architect's Work Lives on in Grand Mansions," *Dallas Times Herald*, October 10, 1983, pp. 1E, 16E.

19. Davis and Grobe, *The Encyclopedia of Texas*, p. 695.

20. Interview with Maybelle Lemmon and Dr. Mark Lemmon, September 21, 1979.

21. Carolyn Hewes Toft, *St. Louis: Landmarks and Historic Districts* (St. Louis: Landmarks Association of St. Louis, Inc., 2002), p. 54.

22. Ruth Patterson Maddox, *Building SMU: 1915–1957* (Dallas: Odenwald Press, 1995), pp. 15–17.

23. Jay C. Henry, *Architecture in Texas: 1895–1945* (Austin: University of Texas Press, 1993), p. 142.

24. Lemmon's personal library included a monograph that he purchased in 1924: Bertram Grosvenor Goodhue, *A Book of Architectural and Decorative Drawings* (New York: Architectural Book Publishing Company, 1924). In addition, there was another fine monograph on the firm's work available during the mid-1920s: Charles Harris Whitaker, ed., *Bertram Grosvenor Goodhue—Architect and Master of Many Arts* (New York: Architectural Book Publishing Company, 1925).

25. Interview with Maybelle Lemmon and Dr. Mark Lemmon, September 21, 1979.

26. In the *Yearbook 1922: First Annual Exhibition of the Dallas Architectural Club*, the following projects by Mark Lemmon and De Witt and Lemmon were published: H. Holmes Green Residence, Julius Shapiro Residence, Foster Apartments, and an Apartment House for the SMU Theological Department. Harper and Annie Kirby Hall at SMU was published in *Architectural Forum* (June 1926). The Municipal Auditorium Competition entry was published in *American Architect–Architectural Review* (May 1925). A Four-unit Apartment Building in Dallas was published in *Architectural Forum* (September 1925). The Goliad School in Galveston was published in *Architectural Record* (May 1926) and in *Architectural Forum* (March 1928).

27. John W. Reps, *Cities of the American West: A History of Frontier American Planning* (Princeton, N.J.: Princeton University Press, 1979), pp. 605–607.

28. G. M. Sims, "Resume of the Early History of the Port Arthur School System" (http://www.paisd.org/history.html, accessed July 6, 2004).

29. Interview with Melzia MacIver, October 13, 1979.

30. See, for example, Georgian Revival high schools in Rhode Island, New York, Delaware, Maryland, Michigan, and Ohio published in C. W. Short and R. Stanley Brown, *Public Buildings: Architecture under the Public Works Administration, 1933–1939, Volume 1* (Washington, D.C.: U.S. General Printing Office, 1939), pp. 191–211.

31. During the summer of 1926, while on one of his many European travels, Mark Lemmon purchased in Venice the following book: Corrado Ricci, *L'Architettura Romanica in Italia* (Stuttgart, Germany: Julius Hoffman Editore, 1925). In 1927 Frank Kean purchased the English edition of this same book, which was also published in 1925 by William Heinemann, Ltd., of London.

32. Henry-Russell Hitchcock, *Modern Architecture: Romanticism and Reintegration* (London: Payson and Clark, 1929), p. 103.

33. Fuller, ed., *AIA Guide to Dallas Architecture*, p. 51.

34. Interviews with Frank Kean, November 2, 1979, and Louis Fuertes, January 8, 1980.

35. The other architects on Mark Lemmon's team were Clyde Griesenbeck and George Marble.

36. Henry, *Architecture in Texas: 1895–1945*, pp. 197–198.

37. For a discussion of Cret's work, see Elizabeth Greenwell Grossman, *The Civic Architecture of Paul Cret* (Cambridge: Cambridge University Press, 1996). For a discussion of the U.S. Courthouse in Fort Worth, see Judith Singer Cohen, *Cowtown Moderne: Art Deco Architecture of Fort Worth, Texas* (College Station: Texas A&M University Press, 1988), pp. 113–119.

38. Ralph Adams Cram established his first office with Francis Wentworth in Boston in 1880. Bertram Goodhue, who had recently won a national architectural competition for the St. Matthews Episcopal Cathedral in Dallas, joined with Cram & Wentworth in 1892, and soon after became their partner. When Wentworth died in 1899, the firm became Cram, Goodhue, & Ferguson. Goodhue moved from Boston in 1903 to open the firm's New York office. The two architects collaborated rarely after this date, in essence, functioning as two independent offices, even competing with one another for the same projects. In 1914, Goodhue withdrew from his partnership with Cram to establish his own practice in New York. He died in 1924.

39. See D. J. R. Bruckner and Irene Macauley, eds., *Dreams in Stone: The University of Chicago* (Chicago: University of Chicago, 1976), pp. 187–192, and Jean F. Block, *The Uses of Gothic: Planning and Building the Campus of the University of Chicago 1892–1932* (Chicago: University of Chicago Library, 1983), pp. 152–161.

40. Interview with Louis Fuertes, January 8, 1980.

41. "Record Poll in Dallas Produces Wide Variety of Choices," *Architectural Record*, August 1940, pp. 22–23.

42. See *The Campus Guide* series published by Princeton University Press, with separate architectural guides to the Harvard and Yale campuses.

43. See Terry Friedman, *James Gibbs* (New Haven, Conn.: Yale University Press, 1984), pp. 54–85.

44. Paul Philippe Cret, "Report Accompanying the General Plan of Development" (unpublished), January 1933, pp. 18–19.

45. Williamson, "A History of the Campus and Buildings of the University of Texas with Emphasis on the Sources for the Architectural Styles," p. 54.

46. Lynn Landrum, "Thinking Out Loud," *The Dallas Morning News*, November 26, 1949, p. III-5.

47. Ibid.

48. See Paolo Berdini, *Walter Gropius: Works and Projects* (Barcelona: Editorial Gustavo Gilli, S.A., 1994), pp. 205–207.

49. Dawson Duncan, "University Building Plan Draws Student Attack," *The Dallas Morning News*, November 23, 1949, p. III-2.

50. Ibid.

51. Landrum, "Thinking Out Loud," p. III-5.

52. For a survey of mid-century school design, see Wolf Von Eckardt, ed., *Mid-Century Architecture in America*

BUILDINGS AND PROJECTS
by De Witt and Lemmon, and Mark Lemmon

Compiled by Willis Cecil Winters, 2004

For a complete list of a building's illustrations, please refer to the index.

MARK LEMMON (WHILE EMPLOYED
BY HAL THOMSON) 1919–1921

1919–1920
H. Holmes Green Residence
6119 Bryan Pkwy.
Dallas

1920–1921
Julius Shapiro Residence
2515 Forest Ave. (M. L. King Jr., Blvd.)
Dallas

DE WITT AND LEMMON 1921–1926

1921–1922
Stephen F. Austin Elementary School
Washington Ave. and Gaston Ave.
Dallas
Demolished

1921
Foster Apartments
Dallas
Not Built

1921
Apartment House for Theological Department
Southern Methodist University, University Park
Dallas
Not Built

1921–1927
First Unit and Administration Building
Methodist Hospital, 301 W. Colorado Blvd.
Dallas
Demolished

1922–1923
Overland Automobile Co. Building
S. Ervay St. and Cadiz St.
Dallas
Demolished

Plate 18
*Brick pattern detail from Woodrow
Wilson High School,* Dallas,
1925–1929.

1922–1924

Goliad Junior High School

with William B. Ittner, St. Louis

Galveston

Condition Unknown

(figure 21, page 34)

1922–1924

Elementary School

with William B. Ittner, St. Louis

Galveston

Condition Unknown

1923–1924

Central High School

with William B. Ittner, St. Louis

2627 Avenue M

Galveston

Renovated as Old Central Cultural Center

(figure 62)

1923–1924

School

Galveston

Condition Unknown

Fig. 62
Central High School, Galveston.

1923–1924

Mark Lemmon Residence

3211 Mockingbird Ln., University Park

Dallas

(plates 19–21)

1923–1924

Harper and Annie Kirby Hall (later renamed
Fred Florence Hall)

Southern Methodist University, University Park

Dallas

(figure 23, page 37)

1923–1925

Sunset High School

2120 W. Jefferson Blvd.

Dallas

(figure 20, page 33)

1924

Municipal Auditorium

Dallas

Competition Entry—Not Built

Plate 19
Mark Lemmon Residence, Dallas.

Plate 20
Window detail from
Mark Lemmon Residence, Dallas.

Plate 21
Entry hall from
Mark Lemmon Residence, Dallas.

1924–1925

Central High School Addition

2627 Avenue M

Galveston

Renovated as Old Central Cultural Center

1924–1925

San Jacinto Elementary School

1100 Moody

Galveston

Condition Unknown

1924–1925

Raynal School

Denison

Condition Unknown

1924–1926

Junior High School

404 E. 22nd St.

Cameron, Texas

Condition Unknown

1924–1926

Negro School

Cameron

Condition Unknown

1924–1925

Apartment Building

Oak Lawn Ave. and Hall St.

Dallas

Demolished

1925–1926

George T. Reynolds Residence

4216 Armstrong Pkwy., Highland Park

Dallas

(plate 22)

1925–1926

Jordan C. Ownby Stadium

Southern Methodist University, University Park

Dallas

Demolished

(figure 63)

Fig. 63
Jordan C. Ownby Stadium, Dallas.

Plate 22
George T. Reynolds Residence, Dallas.

1925–1926
Peabody School
Denison
Condition Unknown

1925–1926
Will Garonzick Residence
2501 South Blvd.
Dallas

1925–1926
E. P. Craig Residence
Denison
Condition Unknown

1925–1926
Mount Auburn Elementary School Addition
6012 E. Grand Ave.
Dallas

1925–1927
Sanctuary and Sunday School Building
Highland Park United Methodist Church
3300 Mockingbird Ln., University Park
Dallas
(figure 26, page 41)

1925–1929
Woodrow Wilson High School
100 S. Glasgow Dr.
Dallas
(plates 23–25)

1926–1927
Denison High School Addition
Denison
Condition Unknown

Plate 23
Opposite page: *Architectural graphics from Woodrow Wilson High School*, Dallas.

Plate 24
*Entry and decorative detailing
from Woodrow Wilson
High School*, Dallas.

Plate 25
*Roof and decorative detailing
from Woodrow Wilson
High School*, Dallas.

MARK LEMMON 1926–1965

1926
Texas School Book Depository
Dallas
Not Built

1926–1928
Education Building
Highland Park Presbyterian Church,
    3821 University Blvd., University Park
Dallas

1927–1929
Thomas Jefferson High School
2200 Twelfth St.
Port Arthur
Condition Unknown
(figure 27, page 45)

1927–1928
Port Acres School
Port Arthur
Condition Unknown

1927–1928
Lamar School (Lamar Guidance Center)
501 W. 17th St.
Port Arthur
Condition Unknown

1927–1928
Lincoln School (Memorial High School)
1023 Abe Lincoln Ave.
Port Arthur

1927–1928
Stephen F. Austin Junior High School Addition
2441 61st St.
Port Arthur

1927–1928
Robert E. Lee Elementary School Addition
3939 Delaware St.
Port Arthur

1927–1929
Edgemore School
Delaware Ave. and Braley St.
Port Arthur
Condition Unknown

1927–1929
Tyrrell Elementary School Addition
4401 Ferndale Dr.
Port Arthur
(figure 28, page 45)

1928–1929
Sunday School Building
First Presbyterian Church
Ardmore, Oklahoma
Condition Unknown

1928–1930
Fair Park Stadium (Cotton Bowl)
Dallas
Extensive Alterations and Additions
(figure 64)

1929

J. M. Maroney Residence

Highland Park

Dallas

Not Built

1929–1930

North Dallas High School Addition

3120 N. Haskell Ave.

Dallas

1929–1931

Third Church of Christ Scientist

4419 Oak Lawn Ave.

Dallas

(plates 26–29)

Fig. 64
Fair Park Stadium (Cotton Bowl),
Dallas.

Plate 26
Third Church of Christ Scientist,
Dallas.

Plate 27
Sanctuary in Third Church of Christ Scientist, Dallas.

Plate 28
*Tower Stairwell in Third Church
of Christ Scientist,* Dallas.

Plate 29
*Roof and decorative detail from Third
Church of Christ Scientist,* Dallas.

1929–1931

Tower Petroleum Building

Elm St. and St. Paul St.

Dallas

(plates 30 and 31)

1930–1932

West District Negro Elementary School

with Donald N. McKenzie, Galveston

35th St. and N St.

Galveston

Condition Unknown

Plate 30
Decorative detail from
Tower Petroleum Building, Dallas.

Plate 31
Tower Petroleum Building Façade,
Dallas.

1931–1933

Boude Storey Junior High School

3000 Maryland Ave.

Dallas

(plates 32 and 33)

1931–1933

Longview Senior High School

Longview

Condition Unknown

Plate 32
Boude Storey Junior High School, Dallas.

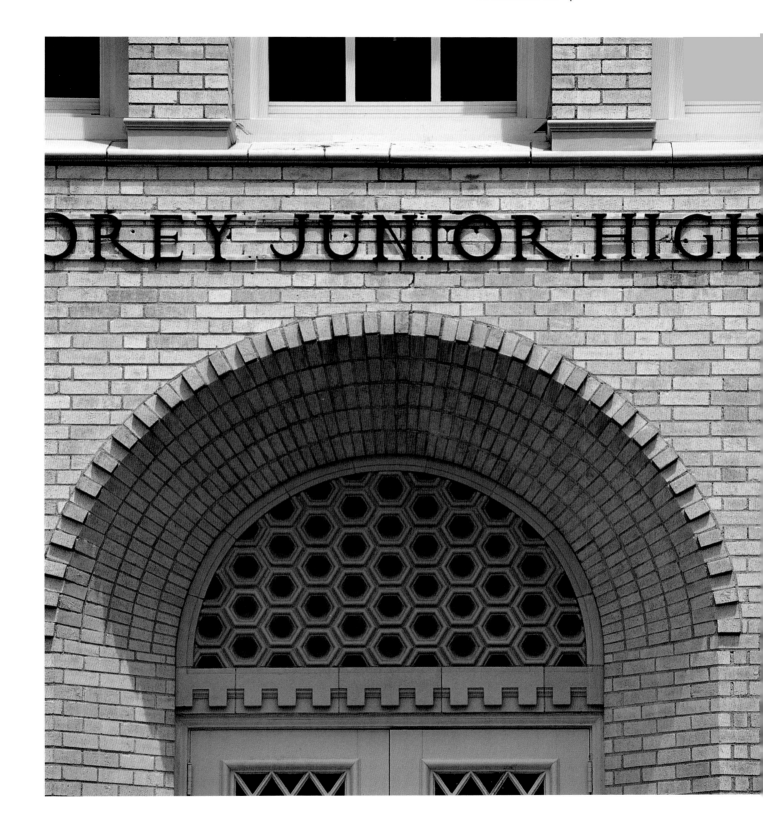

Plate 33
*Door and graphic detail from Boude
Storey Junior High School,* Dallas.

1933–1939

Junior College Building

Hockaday School

Greenville Ave. at Belmont Ave.

Dallas

Demolished

(figure 65)

1935

Henry Catto Residence

3200 Mockingbird Ln., University Park

Dallas

Not Built

1935–1936

Charles H. Warren Residence

Northwest Hwy.

Dallas

Demolished

1935–1936

Stephen F. Austin Junior High School Addition

2441 61st St.

Port Arthur

Fig. 65
Junior College Building, Hockaday
School, Dallas.

Fig. 66
Fine Arts Building, Texas State
College for Women, Denton.

1935–1936

Fine Arts Building

with Hal Thomson

Texas State College for Women

Denton

Condition Unknown

(figure 66)

1935–1936

J. E. Langwith Elementary School

700 N. Catherine St.

Terrell

1935–1936

Physical Education Building

Thomas Jefferson High School

2200 Jefferson Dr.

Port Arthur

Condition Unknown

1935–1936

Great National Life Insurance Co. Office

Building Renovation

with Grayson Gill

1610 Main St.

Dallas

Demolished

1935–1936

Dallas Museum of Natural History

with C. H. Griesenbeck and John Danna

Fair Park

Dallas

(figure 34, page 52)

1935–1936

State of Texas Building (Hall of State)

with Texas Centennial Architects and

Adams & Adams, San Antonio

Fair Park

Dallas

(figures 32 and 33, page 51)

1935–1936

Arlington Hall

Lee Park

Dallas

1935–1936

Base and Exedra for Robert E. Lee Equestrian Statue

Lee Park

Dallas

(figure 68)

1936–1937

Florence Nightingale Maternity Hospital

Baylor University Hospital

Gaston Ave. and Adair St.

Dallas

Demolished

1936–1937

Dr. W. Lee Hudson Residence

Highland Park

Dallas

Not Built

1936–1937

U.S. Post Office

431 N. Graham St.

Stephenville, Texas

(figure 38, page 56)

1936–1937

Woodrow Wilson Junior High School

1500 Lakeshore Dr.

Port Arthur

(figure 49, page 67)

1936–1937

William Morris Residence

Chatham Hill Rd. and Douglas Ave.

Dallas

Condition Unknown

Fig. 67
*Base and Exedra for Robert E. Lee
Equestrian Statue*, Lee Park, Dallas.

1936–1937

Mrs. R. R. Penn Ranch House

Duncanville, Texas

Condition Unknown

1936–1937

Angus Wynne Residence Guest House

Strait Ln.

Dallas

Condition Unknown

1935–1936

Morton H. Marr Residence Renovation

Inwood Rd. and Park Ln.

Dallas

Condition Unknown

1936–1937

Frank W. Hall Residence

Georgetown

Condition Unknown

1936–1937

Dr. B. A. Knickerbocker Residence

3430 Rankin Ave., University Park

Dallas

1936–1937

Cokesbury Book Store

1910 Main St.

Dallas

Demolished

(figure 35, page 53)

1936–1937

Methodist Publishing Co. Office Interiors

Cokesbury Book Store Building

1910 Main St.

Dallas

Demolished

1936–1938

Percy R. Knickerbocker Residence

3608 Rosedale Ave.

Dallas

Demolished

1937–1938

Perkins Hall of Administration Addition

Southern Methodist University, University Park

Dallas

1937–1941

Sanctuary

Highland Park Presbyterian Church

3821 University Blvd., University Park

Dallas

(plates 34–37)

1938–1939

Education Building Addition

Gaston Avenue Baptist Church (Criswell Institute)

4024 Gaston Ave.

Dallas

1938–1939

Frank L. McNeny Residence

4422 Belfort Ave., Highland Park

Dallas

Plate 34
*Highland Park Presbyterian Church
Sanctuary*, Dallas.

Plate 35
*Entry detail of Highland Park Presby
Church Sanctuary, Dallas.*

Plate 36
*Altar of Highland Park Presbyterian
Church Sanctuary,* Dallas.

Plate 37
*Side windows of Highland Park
Presbyterian Church Sanctuary,* Dallas.

1938–1939

Jalonick Building (Culwell & Son)

Hillcrest Rd. and McFarlin Blvd., University Park

Dallas

1938–1939

Washington School

815 S. Travis St.

Sherman

Condition Unknown

1938–1940

Alex W. Spence Junior High School

4001 Capitol Ave.

Dallas

(plates 38 and 39)

1939

Jalonick Country House Renovation

Fin and Feather Club

Hutchins

Condition Unknown

Plate 38
Alex W. Spence Junior High School, Dallas.

Plate 39
*Window detail from Alex W. Spence
Junior High School*, Dallas.

1939–1940
Tyrrell Elementary School Addition
4401 Ferndale
Port Arthur
Condition Unknown

1939–1941
Dallas Talmud Torah and Menorah Institute
Park St. and Eakin St.
Dallas
Demolished

1940–1942
Frazier Courts Public Housing
4600 Spring Ave.
Dallas
Rebuilt with support from the Foundation for
    Community Empowerment

1940–1942
Joe Perkins Gymnasium
Southern Methodist University, University Park
Dallas
Renovated into Natatorium in 1957

1940–1949
Robert S. Hyer Elementary School
3920 Caruth Blvd., University Park
Dallas

1941
Nurses' Home and Education Building
Baylor University Hospital
Dallas
Not Built

1941
Nightingale Maternity Hospital Addition
Baylor University Hospital
Dallas
Not Built

1941–1942
Science Building and Gymnasium
Terrell High School
Terrell
Condition Unknown

1942
San Angelo Air Force Base Advanced Flying School
Robert G. Carr Municipal Airport
San Angelo
Condition Unknown

1944
Student Activities Building
Southern Methodist University, University Park
Dallas
Not Built

1944
Chemistry Building
Southern Methodist University, University Park
Dallas
Not Built

1944–1945

Junior High School

Grand Prairie, Texas

Condition Unknown

1944–1945

Preston Hollow Elementary School

6423 Walnut Hill Ln.

Dallas

(figure 68)

1944–1946

Sanctuary, Chapel, and Youth Center

First Methodist Church, Beauregard Ave.

San Angelo

(figure 69)

Fig. 68
Preston Hollow Elementary School,
Dallas.

Fig. 69
First Methodist Church,
San Angelo.

1944–1948

Second Education Building

Highland Park Presbyterian Church

3821 University Blvd., University Park

Dallas

1945

Cotton Bowl (New Stadium), Fair Park

Dallas

Not Built

1945

Education Building Addition

First Methodist Church

Beauregard Ave.

San Angelo

1945–1947

Elementary School

Grand Prairie, Texas

Condition Unknown

1945–1947

Highland Park Junior High School Addition
*   (McCulloch Intermediate School)*

3520 Normandy Ave., Highland Park

Dallas

1945–1947

Farm & Home Savings and Loan Building

1210 Main St.

Dallas

Demolished

1945–1949

Education Building Addition

Highland Park Presbyterian Church

3821 University Blvd., University Park

Dallas

1946

Agriculture Building

Southern Methodist University, University Park

Dallas

Not Built

1946

Texas Research Foundation Laboratory

Dallas

Not Built

1946

Herbert Marcus Fine Arts Building

Hockaday School

Dallas

Not Built

1946–1947

Sparks Clinic and Hospital Addition

5003 Ross Ave.

Dallas

Demolished

1946–1948

Caruth Engineering Building

Southern Methodist University, University Park

Dallas

1946–1948

Robert E. Lee Elementary School Addition

3939 Delaware St.

Port Arthur

1946–1950

Fondren Science Building

Southern Methodist University, University Park

Dallas

(plates 40–42)

1946–1950

Sanctuary

Gaston Avenue Baptist Church (Criswell Institute)

4024 Gaston Ave.

Dallas

1947–1948

Wilkinson Clinic

101 N. Zang Blvd.

Dallas

1947–1949

Wynnewood Presbyterian Church

2324 S. Vernon Ave.

Dallas

Plate 40
Fondren Science Building, Southern
Methodist University, Dallas.

Plate 41
Window detail from Fondren Science Building, Southern Methodist University, Dallas.

Plate 42
Roof detail from Fondren Science Building,
Southern Methodist University, Dallas.

1947–1949
First Presbyterian Church
230 W. Rusk Ave.
Tyler

1947–1949
Harper & Annie Kirby Hall (Fred Florence Hall)
    Renovation and Addition
Southern Methodist University, University Park
Dallas

1947–1949
Hillcrest High School Addition
9924 Hillcrest Rd.
Dallas

1947–1950
B. H. Macon Elementary School
650 Holcomb Rd.
Dallas

1947–1951
Roy H. Laird Memorial Hospital
Henderson Blvd. and Dudley Rd.
Kilgore
Condition Unknown

1947–1951
Perkins Chapel
Southern Methodist University, University Park
Dallas
(plates 43 and 44)

Plate 43
Perkins Chapel, Southern Methodist
University, Dallas.

Plate 44
Mid-tower detail from Perkins Chapel,
Southern Methodist University, Dallas.

1947–1951

Bridwell Library

Southern Methodist University, University Park

Dallas

(figure 70)

1947–1951

Harper and Annie Kirby Hall

Southern Methodist University, University Park

Dallas

1947–1951

A. Frank Smith Hall

Southern Methodist University, University Park

Dallas

1947–1951

S. B. Perkins Hall Dormitory

Southern Methodist University, University Park

Dallas

1947–1951

Paul E. Martin Hall Apartments

Southern Methodist University, University Park

Dallas

1947–1951

Eugene B. Hawk Hall Apartments

Southern Methodist University, University Park

Dallas

Fig. 70
Bridwell Library, Southern Methodist
University, Dallas.

1947–1952
Wynne Chapel
Highland Park Presbyterian Church
3821 University Blvd., University Park
Dallas

1948–1949
Cokesbury Book Store Addition
1909 Commerce St.
Dallas
Demolished

1948–1950
Peyton Hall Dormitory
Southern Methodist University, University Park
Dallas

1948–1950
Lone Star Gas Co. Building
1824 Wood St.
Dallas
Renovated as First Presbyterian Church Children's
    Education Center

1948–1951
Presbyterian Bookstore
1814 Main St.
Dallas
Demolished

1948–1951
Stephen F. Austin Junior High School Addition
2441 61st St.
Port Arthur

1948–1951
Tyrrell Elementary School Addition
4401 Ferndale Dr.
Port Arthur

1948–1951
Southwestern Legal Center (Robert G. Storey Hall)
Southern Methodist University, University Park
Dallas
(figure 55, page 72)

1948–1951
Lawyers Inn (Carr P. Collins Hall)
Southern Methodist University, University Park
Dallas

1949
Lower School Addition and Dormitory
St. Mark's School of Texas
Dallas
Not Built

1949
Student Union Building
University of Texas Medical Branch
Galveston
Not Built

1949–1951
Robert S. Hyer Elementary School Addition
3920 Caruth Blvd., University Park
Dallas

1949–1951

Platter Methodist Church (Waples Memorial United Methodist Church)

830 W. Main St.

Denison

1949–1951

Gamma Phi Beta Sorority House

3030 Daniel Ave.

Southern Methodist University, University Park

Dallas

1949–1951

Covenant Presbyterian Church (First Family Church)

9353 Garland Rd.

Dallas

1949–1951

American Liberty Oil Co. Building Renovation and Addition

3417 Gillespie Ave.

Dallas

Renovated as The Mansion on Turtle Creek

1949–1951

DeQueen Elementary School Addition

740 DeQueen Blvd.

Port Arthur

1949–1951

Lincoln School Addition (Memorial High School)

1023 Abe Lincoln Ave.

Port Arthur

Fig. 71
St. Luke's Methodist Church, Houston.

Fig. 72
Batts Hall, University of Texas, Austin.

1949–1951

Perkins Dry Goods Co. Building

708 Jackson St.

Dallas

Demolished

1949–1951

Lone Star Steel Co. Building

Daingerfield

Condition Unknown

1949–1951

Smith Electric Co. Building

3200 Grand Ave.

Dallas

1949–1951

Rosemont Elementary School Boiler Room Addition

719 N Montclair Ave.

Dallas

1949–1951

St. Luke's Methodist Church

3471 Westheimer Rd.

Houston

(figure 71)

1949–1952

*Urban Park Elementary School Auditorium
and Classroom Addition*

6901 Military Pkwy.

Dallas

1949–1952

Batts Hall

The University of Texas

Austin

(figure 72)

1949–1952

Mezes Hall

The University of Texas

Austin

1949–1952

Benedict Hall

The University of Texas

Austin

(figure 73)

1949–1952

San Jacinto Elementary School

7900 Hume Dr.

Dallas

1949–1952

W. E. Greiner Junior High School Annex

625 S. Edgefield Ave.

Dallas

Fig. 73
Benedict Hall, University of Texas,
Austin.

1950–1952

Education Building

Preston Hollow Presbyterian Church

9800 Preston Rd.

Dallas

1950–1953

Townes Hall

The University of Texas

Austin

1951

Religious Activities Building

Southern Methodist University, University Park

Dallas

Not Built

1951–1953

Casa View Elementary School

2100 Farola Dr.

Dallas

(figure 57, page 76)

1951–1953

Holy Rosary Catholic Church

1416 George St.

Rosenberg

1951–1953

Wilkinson Clinic Addition

101 N. Zang Blvd.

Dallas

1951–1954

St. Luke's Methodist Church Addition

3471 Westheimer Rd.

Houston

1952–1954

Selecman Hall

Southern Methodist University, University Park

Dallas

1952–1954

Joseph Wylie Fincher Memorial Building

Southern Methodist University, University Park

Dallas

(figure 56, page 73)

1952–1954

Hillcrest High School Addition

9924 Hillcrest Rd.

Dallas

1952–1954

First Baptist Church

2104 W. Louisiana St.

Midland

Condition Unknown

1952–1955

Cary Basic Sciences Building

The University of Texas Southwestern
     Medical Center

Dallas

(figure 59, page 81)

1953–1955

Municipal Building Annex

with Smith & Mills

2014 Main St.

Dallas

1953–1955

*Dallas Country Club Clubhouse Renovation
    and Addition*

Mockingbird Ln., Highland Park

Dallas

1953

Student Union

The University of Texas Medical Branch

Galveston

Project

1953

Dormitories and Apartments

The University of Texas Medical Branch

Galveston

Project

1953–1955

Preston Hollow Elementary School

6423 Walnut Hill Ln.

Dallas

1953–1955

Pleasant Grove Elementary School

1614 N. St. Augustine Rd.

Dallas

1954

Sanctuary

Highland Park United Methodist Church,
    University Park

Dallas

Project

1954

Highland Park Town Hall Addition

4700 Drexel Dr., Highland Park

Dallas

1954–1958

Southland Center

with Welton Becket and Associates, Los Angeles

400 Olive St.

Dallas

Renovated as the Adams Mark Hotel

1954–1956

Albert Sydney Johnston Elementary School

2020 Mouser St.

Dallas

1954–1956

John Ireland Elementary School

1515 Jim Miller Rd.

Dallas

1954–1956

Rufus Burleson Elementary School

6300 Elam Rd.

Dallas

1954–1956

Olmstead-Kirk Paper Co. Graphic Arts Center

2420 Butler St.

Dallas

Demolished

1954–1957

W. W. Samuell High School

8928 Palisade Dr.

Dallas

(plate 45)

1955–1957

Shuttles Hall

Southern Methodist University, University Park

Dallas

Plate 45
W.W. Samuell High School, Dallas.

1955–1957

Joe Perkins Natatorium Renovation

Southern Methodist University, University Park

Dallas

1955–1957

St. Luke's Methodist Church Addition

3471 Westheimer Rd.

Houston

1955–1957

Second Education Building and Gym

Preston Hollow Presbyterian Church

9800 Preston Rd.

Dallas

1955–1958

Kinsolving Hall Women's Dormitory

The University of Texas

Austin

1955–1958

Hoblitzelle Clinical Sciences Building

The University of Texas Southwestern

    Medical Center

Dallas

(figure 59, page 81)

1956–1958

Braniff Airlines Operations Center

with Pereira & Luckman, Los Angeles

7701 Lemmon Ave., Love Field

Dallas

1956–1962

First Presbyterian Church

Taft Blvd. and Harrison St.

Wichita Falls

(figure 60, page 82)

1957–1959

Mary Hay Hall

Southern Methodist University, University Park

Dallas

1957–1959

Churchill Way Presbyterian Church

12330 Preston Rd.

Dallas

Renovated as the Cooper Clinic

1957–1959

St. Philip's Catholic Church and School

8151 Military Pkwy.

Dallas

1958–1959

Umphrey Lee Cenotaph

Southern Methodist University, University Park

Dallas

(figure 74)

1958–1960

St. Augustine Catholic Church

1047 N. St. Augustine Dr.

Dallas

1958–1960

J. L. Long Junior High School Addition

6116 Reiger Ave.

Dallas

Fig. 74
Umphrey Lee Cenotaph, Southern
Methodist University, Dallas.

1959–1960

Mrs. Ernest MacIver Residence

551 Northlake Dr.

Dallas

1959–1961

Casa View Elementary School Addition

2100 Farola Dr.

Dallas

1959–1961

John Quincy Adams Elementary School Addition

8239 Lake June Rd.

Dallas

1959–1961

Reinhardt Elementary School Addition

10122 Losa Dr.

Dallas

1959–1963

Federal Building (Earle Cabell Federal Building)

with George Dahl

1100 Commerce St.

Dallas

1959–1961

Education Building Addition

Highland Park United Methodist Church

3300 Mockingbird Ln., University Park

Dallas

1959–1961

Edwin J. Kiest Elementary School Addition

2611 Healey Dr.

Dallas

1960–1962

Sanctuary

Preston Hollow Presbyterian Church

9800 Preston Rd.

Dallas

1961–1964

Moody Memorial First Methodist Church

2803 53rd St.

Galveston

(figure 61, page 82)

1962

West Building

Highland Park Presbyterian Church

3821 University Blvd., University Park

Dallas

Project

1962–1965

Third Education Building

Highland Park Presbyterian Church

3821 University Blvd., University Park

Dallas

Plate 46
*Fireplace and wood storage at
Mark Lemmon residence*, Dallas,
1923–1924.

Compiled by Julie Bagley

WORKS THAT CITE MARK LEMMON

American Institute of Architects, Dallas Chapter, John H. Box, Chairman. *The Prairie's Yield: Forces Shaping Dallas Architecture from 1840 to 1962.* New York: Reinhold Publishing Corporation, 1962, pp. 30, 31, 38, 39, 46, 67, and 76.

American Institute of Architects, Dallas Chapter, Larry Paul Fuller, ed. *Guide to Dallas Architecture with Regional Highlights.* Dallas: McGraw-Hill Construction Information Group, 1999, pp. 26, 27, 43, 46, 52, 53, 60, 112, 125, 126, 127, and 146.

American Institute of Architects, Dallas Chapter, Alan R. Sumner, ed. *Dallasights: An Anthology of Architecture and Open Spaces.* Dallas: Dallas Chapter, American Institute of Architects, 1978, pp. 50, 77, and 158.

Bagley, Julie. "Dallas as Region: Mark Lemmon's Gothic Revival Highland Park Presbyterian Church." Thesis for Master of Arts, University of North Texas, August 2004.

Butler, Steve. "Honoring the Past: Confederate Monuments in Dallas." *Legacies: A History Journal for Dallas and North Central Texas* 1, no. 2 (Fall 1989): 31–36.

Collier, Diane M. Hospodka. "Art Deco Architecture: Dallas, Texas." Thesis for Master of Architecture, University of Texas at Arlington, December 1980.

Cox, Tezzie J. *The Christian Message in Stained Glass: Highland Park Presbyterian Church.* Dallas: Taylor Publishing Company, 1991.

Dillon, David. *Dallas Architecture: 1936–1986.* Austin: Texas Monthly Press, 1985, pp. 16, 31, and 36.

——. *Dallas in Context: Architecture since 1945.* Dallas: Heritage Press, 1986.

——. "Grandly Gothic: Architect Mark Lemmon Left Dallas a Legacy That Reflects His Love of Tradition." *Dallas Morning News,* January 14, 1989, 1C.

——. "Who Built This Place? Forgotten Architects Gave Dallas Some Quirky Character." *Dallas Morning News,* May 2, 1999, 8C.

Holden, Thomas S., ed. "Christian Scientists Use Romanesque." *Architectural Record* 83, no. 4 (April 1938): 57–60.

Plate 47
Tower detail from Third Church of Christ Scientist, Dallas, 1929–1931.

——. "With Record Readers: Record Poll in Dallas Produces Wide Variety of Choices." *Architectural Record* 88, no. 2 (August 1940): 16–18.

Long, Christopher. "Lemmon, Mark," *The Handbook of Texas Online,* 2002. Accessed September 13, 2003, from http://www.tsha.utexas.edu/handbook/online.html.

MacDougall, A. E. "New Features in Apartment House Buildings." *Architectural Forum* 3, no. 3 (September 1925): 163–64.

Maddox, Ruth Patterson. *Building SMU: 1915–1957, A Warm and Personal Look at the People Who Started Southern Methodist University.* Dallas: Odenwald Press, 1995.

Myers, Howard, ed. "Cokesbury Bookstore, Dallas, Texas: Mark Lemmon, Architect." *Architectural Forum* 67, no. 3 (September 1937): 190–91.

Robinson, Willard. *Reflections of Faith: Houses of Worship in the Lone Star State.* Waco, Tex.: Baylor University Press, 1994, pp. 200–202.

Saxon, Gerald D., and Maxine Holmes, eds. *The WPA Dallas Guide and History: Written and Compiled from 1936 to 1942 by the Writer's Program of the Works Progress Administration in the City of Dallas.* Denton: University of North Texas Press, 1992, pp. 203, 373, and 391.

Study, Guy. "Elementary School Buildings." *Architectural Record* 59, no. 5 (May 1926): 411–14.

"The Cokesbury Book Store, Dallas, Texas: Mark Lemmon, Architect." *Architectural Digest* 10, no. 3 (July 1939): 148–49.

"The Hockaday School, Dallas, Texas: Mark Lemmon, Architect." *Architectural Digest* 10, no. 3 (July 1939): 145–47.

Thrower, Frank, AIA, and Marian Ann J. Montgomery, Ph.D. "Mark Lemmon: Dallas Architect of Community Churches." Unpublished manuscript, 2003, Highland Park Presbyterian Church Archives, Dallas.

Tyler, Ron, et al., eds. *New Handbook of Texas,* vol. 2. Austin: Texas State Historical Association, 1996.

Waterbury, Harry S. "Designing and Planning Laboratory Buildings." *Architectural Forum* 44, no. 6 (June 1926): 393–94.

White, James F. *Architecture at SMU: 50 Years and Buildings.* Dallas: Southern Methodist University, 1966.

Williams, Peter. *Houses of God: Region, Religion, and Architecture in the United States.* Chicago: University of Illinois Press, 1997.

Winters, Willis. "The Architecture of Mark Lemmon 1920–1968." Unpublished research, University of Texas, 1979, Meadows Museum, Southern Methodist University, Dallas.

——. "Mark Lemmon." From "A Texas Fifty," ed. Joel Barna. *Texas Architect* 39, no. 6 (November–December 1989): 33–81.

WORKS RELEVANT TO TEXAS/DALLAS/REVIVAL ARCHITECTURE

Acheson, Sam. *Dallas Yesterday.* Dallas: Southern Methodist University Press, 1977.

Driskill, Frank, and Noel Grisham. *Historic Churches of Texas: The Land and the People.* Burnett, Tex.: Eakin Press, 1980.

Greene, A. C. *Dallas: The Deciding Years: A Historical Portrait.* Austin, Texas: Encino Press, 1973.

Hazel, Michael. *Dallas: A History of Big D.* Austin: Texas State Historical Association, 1997.

Henry, Jay C. *Architecture in Texas: 1895–1945.* Austin: University of Texas Press, 1993.

Leslie, Warren. *Dallas Public and Private.* New York: Grossman Publishers, 1964.

McDonald, William M. *Dallas Rediscovered: A Photographic Chronicle of Urban Expansion, 1870–1925.* Dallas: Dallas Historical Society, 1978.

Ragsdale, Kenneth. *Centennial '36: The Year America Discovered Texas.* College Station: Texas A&M University Press, 1987.

Rogers, John W. *Lusty Texans of Dallas.* New York: E. P. Dutton and Co., Inc., 1951.

Stanton, Phoebe. *The Gothic Revival and American Church Architecture: An Episode in Taste, 1840–1856.* Baltimore: Johns Hopkins Press, 1968.

Steege, Gwen W. "The Book of Plans and Early Romanesque Revival in the United States." *Journal of the Society of Architectural Historians* 46 (September 1987): 215–27.

WORKS THAT LEMMON MAY HAVE DRAWN UPON

Blomfield, Sir Reginald. *A History of French Architecture, Vol. 1: From the Reign of Charles VIII till the Death of Mazarin, 1494 to 1661.* London: G. Bell and Sons, Ltd., 1911.

———. *A History of French Architecture, Vol. 2: From the Death of Mazarin till the death of Louis XV, 1661–1774.* London: G. Bell and Sons, Ltd., 1921.

Connick, Charles. *Adventures in Light and Color: An Introduction to the Stained Glasscraft.* New York: Random House, 1937.

Cram, Ralph Adams. *American Church Building of Today.* New York: Architectural Book Publishing Co., Inc., 1929.

———. *Church Building: A Study of Principles of Architecture in Their Relation to the Church.* Boston: Marshall Jones, 1924.

Eberlein, Harold D., and Cortlandt Van Dyke Hubbard. *Colonial Interiors: Federal and Greek Revival.* Third Series. New York: William Helburn Inc., 1938

Edgell, G. H. *The American Architecture of Today.* New York: Charles Scribner's Sons, 1928.

Morgan, Morris H., translator. *Vitruvius: The Ten Books of Architecture.* Cambridge, Mass.: Harvard University Press, 1926.

Ruskin, John. *The Seven Lamps of Architecture.* Reprint. New York: E. P. Dutton and Co., 1907.

Tallmadge, Thomas E. *The Story of Architecture in America.* New York: W. W. Norton & Company Inc., 1927.

Upjohn, Everard M. *Richard Upjohn: Architect and Churchman.* New York: Colombia University Press, 1939.

Ware, William R. *The Georgian Period: Being Photographs and Measured Drawings of Colonial Work with Text.* Vols. 1 and 2. New York: U.P.C. Book Company, Inc., 1923.

MISCELLANEOUS ARTICLES

"First Unit of Highland Park Presbyterian Church of Dallas, Texas." *Christian Observer* 116, no. 27 (July 4, 1928): 8.

"Pastor Tells of Church's Rapid Growth." *Dallas Times Herald,* September 21, 1938, Section 1, 10.

Ruggles, William B. "Locating the Church." *The Park Cities News,* April 29, 1976, 7C.

INDEX

Page numbers in bold refer to illustrations.

Plate 48
Brick detail from Boude Storey Junior High School, Dallas, 1931–1933.